Praying the Psalms

GW00457014

JOSEPH EDWARDS-HOFF

DEDICATION

First and foremost, I would like to dedicate this book to my wife Nicole and my children. They have borne with me as I have spent time in prayer, in study, in writing, and all of the other works that God has called me to. They have supported me and have been my greatest reminder of my need to pray.

I also want to dedicate this work to the great men of prayer who have inspired my own prayer life. Men like Leonard Ravenhill, E. M. Bounds, R. A. Torrey, George Müller, and more. Their wise counsel and examples for us will be cherished forever.

Lastly, I dedicate this work to the Lord Jesus Christ, to whom I have the privilege to pray to and speak with.

Hear our prayers Lord.

PREFACE

Early in my faith, while attending a men's retreat in the Cascade Mountains of Washington state, I walked out of a session and went back to my room. There I laid on the floor with my face on the ground and I cried out unto God. I had never done anything like that before and He met with me in a special way that day. It was unlike any prayer I had ever prayed before. I cried out to God and He answered me.

For a short season I prayed every morning like that, laying face down on the floor, but as time passed, so did my passion for prayer. Yet God is always faithful and as the years passed, He called me into pastoral ministry and He began to teach me more and more about prayer. I began to read books written by the great saints of old and they inspired me to pray all the more.

I have far from mastered this art of prayer, and I still have my own dry seasons and valleys that I pass through, yet God has impressed it upon my heart that there is no greater task that the believer can undertake than that of prayer. It is so simple that a child can do it, yet so deep that the greatest saint can never master it.

As I began to write these prayers they were for my own keeping, but eventually I believed that they were to be shared in order to stir up a heart for prayer in my brothers and sisters. I hope that they inspire you as you pray them, and moreso that you will be inspired to continue to pray more on your own.

- Pastor Joe

Praying the Psalms

Psalm 1:1-2

Blessed is the man Who walks not in the counsel of the ungodly, Nor stands in the path of sinners, Nor sits in the seat of the scornful; But his delight is in the law of the Lord, And in His law he meditates day and night.

Lord help me be the one who abstains from evil and meditates on Your Word. Father, help me to know Your Word so that I can meditate on it day and night. I can only meditate on what I know. Crucify my flesh and give me a heart that desires to be in Your Word daily. Lord, Your Word will keep me from sinning, or my sin will keep me from Your Word. Let Your Word guide my feet and do not let me sit in the seat of the scornful. Let me set no wicked thing before my eyes and keep me from the temptations that desire to rule over me. Thank You for Your Word Father. It leads me, guides me, and comforts me. Amen.

Psalm 1:3

He shall be like a tree Planted by the rivers of water, that brings forth its fruit in its season, Whose leaf also shall not wither; And whatever he does shall prosper.

Lord, I want to be planted in Your Word. I want my life to be full of the fruit of Your Spirit at work in me. Keep me abiding in Your Word and sensitive to the work of Your Spirit in my life. I desire to bring honor and glory to Your name through all my works. I pray that my hands and feet are used to accomplish Your will and that my conduct always testifies of Your hand at work in my life. Help me to remain faithful in the dry seasons. Help me to trust that You have a plan when my faith seems dry. And forever keep me close to Your side. In Jesus' name.

Psalm 2:1
Why do the nations rage, And the people plot a vain thing?

Oh Lord, I live in a time where people are growing harder
in their hearts. They not only reject Your ways, but they
hate those who follow them. I know that they desire to
follow the lusts of their hearts, but I also know that You can
change the heart of stone. God, I pray that you would soften
the hearts of those around me and that You loose my lips so
that I would speak of Your goodness. I know that Your
goodness can lead them to repentance. Place trials in their
lives and miracles before their eyes. Show them Your love
and Your power. And help me to always be ready to show
them the great hope that You have given me. Bring Your
children home Father. I love You.

Psalm 2:9
You shall break them with a rod of iron;
You shall dash them to pieces like a potter's vessel.

One day Lord, You will reign supreme here on the earth.
Often I wonder, "how long will You let us remain like
this?" But I know that You have a plan and that Your ways
are so incredibly higher than my own ways. When will You
put an end to Evil? When the time of the harvest is
complete! You are so very longsuffering towards us and I
know that when Your plan is complete here on the earth,
You will come and rule and reign. Oh how glorious that day
will be! To see You on the throne and we, Your children,
standing around You worshiping. I long to see Your
kingdom Lord. Help me to live each day in expectancy of
Your coming. Maranatha!

Psalm 2:11-12

Serve the Lord with fear, And rejoice with trembling. *Kiss the Son, lest He be angry, And you perish in the way,* When His wrath is kindled but a little. Blessed are all those who put their trust in Him.

Lord, You are a great dad to me. You lead me, You guide me, and You correct me when I get myself in trouble. Help me to truly have a fear of You in my heart. I want to reverence You. I want to put my trust in You. Today and all days, remind me of Your presence. Holy Spirit, whisper in my ear the moment this world calls out to me with its pleasures. Do not let me wander far. Keep me to Your righteous path. Help me to put my trust in You and to place all things in Your hands. And Jesus, be with me today. Help me to walk as You have shown me. May Your words ever be on my lips. Thank You gracious God, for all that You do for me.

Psalm 3:4

I cried to the Lord with my voice,
And He heard me from His holy hill.

Oh Lord, my head sometimes spins with all that this world throws at me. We live in a day and age of one million distractions. Save me! Only You can keep me and only You can save me from this crazy life. Father, I know that You hear me when I cry out to You. Every time. Please, step down and save me from this world and save me from myself. Hold me in Your loving arms and just assure me that You are on the throne and You hold all things in Your hands. Lord Jesus, I fall before You. I am Yours, save me! Take all that I have and use it for Your glory. Do not let me live for myself any longer. Speak to me continually and keep me in Your ways. Do not let me depart from Your great love. Oh God, You are an awesome God. And You do reign, from heaven above. Thank You for hearing me and for coming to my rescue. Hallelujah, You are King.

Psalm 4:1

Hear me when I call, O God of my righteousness! You have relieved me in my distress; Have mercy on me, and hear my prayer.

O God, to know that You hear me when I call is enough for me. How often I do not feel as if I am worthy of Your attention, yet You hear my every cry. You know what I need, You know what I have done, and You love me still. You show such great mercy to me Father. Your faithfulness is the antonym to my own faithlessness. For every time I have failed, You have proven all the more faithful, loving, and true. Oh God, how You relieve me! I rest in Your presence because I know that You always are near. I sigh with deep breaths of relief in Your presence. Oh Lord my God, You bring me peace.

Psalm 4:3-4

But know that the Lord has set apart for Himself him who is godly; The Lord will hear when I call to Him. Be angry, and do not sin. Meditate within your heart on your bed, and be still.

"Be angry, and do not sin." Oh Father, easier said than done, but I long to please You. I know that You hear me, I know that Your hand is upon me. Lord, give my strength, by Your Holy Spirit, to subdue my passions. Help me not to respond in the flesh and to always have the discerning spirit of Your Son. Jesus, teach me to be quick to hear, slow to speak, and slow to give in to my unrighteous anger. Help me to bridle my tongue. Lord, let all that I say and do be filtered through the guiding of Your Spirit. When I want to give into my flesh, let me hold fast to Your commands, let me trust in Your Word, and help me to move with discernment. Father, I need to seek You morning, noon, and night. I cannot make it through this day without continually drawing from Your wisdom and love. Help me Father. Lord Jesus, lead me. Spirit, fill me afresh that I may bring You glory in all that I do. Hallowed be Your name Lord. Let me live for You.

Psalm 4:8
I will both lie down in peace, and sleep;
For You alone, O Lord, make me dwell in safety.

Oh my Lord, hallowed be Your name. You give me peace
that surpasses understanding. Mind blowing peace! This
world does not know Your peace. They mock and they
sneer at Your promises. But You have been so good to me
Lord. You have shown me Your ways. You have revealed
Your great love for me and You have lead me to meadows
of peace and tranquility through Your Word. The world
does not know the peace You give. To lay down and arise
knowing that Your Spirit is with me. The knowledge of
Your promise, that You work all things to my good. I rest in
Your promises Father. No other thing can give me the peace
that You give. Thank You for saving me and thank You for
Your amazing grace. Oh, what sweet grace. Amen.

Psalm 5:3
My voice You shall hear in the morning, O Lord; In the
morning I will direct it to You, And I will look up.

Lord, give me strength, help me fight against this rebellious
and slothful body of mine and help me to arise early in the
morning to seek You. Help me to have the same spirit as
Your Son. Help me to have the spirit of Your servant David.
Lord. I want to rise early and spend time with You. Lord,
You deserve the firstfruits of my day. I do not want to look
back on my life and see hours of prayer traded for hours of
sleep. Let me live with no regrets. Give me strength Father,
I beg of you.

Psalm 5:7-8

But as for me, I will come into Your house in the multitude of Your mercy; In fear of You I will worship toward Your holy temple. Lead me, O Lord, in Your righteousness because of my enemies; Make Your way straight before my face.

Lord, let me never become wise in my own eyes. Let me never become self-righteous like the Pharisees. Help me come humbly into Your house of mercy. It is not of good that I have done, but by Your Son Jesus alone that I can come before You. It is not of worth or value that I bring, but because of Your love and goodness that I can approach You. Let me reverence You Lord. Let me never take lightly Your holy nature. You are so, so good Lord and so far removed from sin. My mind cannot know the depths of my own depravity, but I know that You are perfect and true. Lead me Lord, for on my own I would never find my way. Teach me Your ways. Teach me how to be righteous and to never bring You shame. Reveal Your will for me. Hide Your Word in my heart and bring understanding to my mind. I live to serve You Father. Receive me, lead me, teach me, and keep me.

Psalm 5:11-12

But let all those rejoice who put their trust in You; Let them ever shout for joy, because You defend them; Let those also who love Your name Be joyful in You. For You, O Lord, will bless the righteous; With favor You will surround him as with a shield.

Father, help me to find my ALL in You. Don't let me look for strength in myself. I need You and You alone. If I look to me, I will fail, but if I look to You Lord, I will never see failure. I can never fail if I am turning my face towards You! Help me believe Father. Help me. It is so easy for me to try to take on this world in my own strength, but I must find my strength in You alone or else I will fall. Give me Your joy. Let me experience Your love. Help me to live like Your Son. Give Your peace that surpasses understanding.

Psalm 6:4

Return, O Lord, deliver me!
Oh, save me for Your mercies' sake!

Lord, I know what I deserve. God, my sin is ever before me and day by day I know how desperately I need You. Lord, please, do have mercy on me because I am so very weak. You know my weakness. You know my frailty. Lord, deliver me for Your mercy's sake! God, do not save me because I am good, save me because You are good. Lord, let Your name be hallowed and exalted in this world because of Your great mercy. Let Your people see Your great love, and mercy, and grace. And Lord, if You find me pleasing before Your sight, use me to show the world Your goodness.

Psalm 6:6-7

I am weary with my groaning; All night I make my bed swim; I drench my couch with my tears. My eye wastes away because of grief; It grows old because of all my enemies.

Oh, Lord God! Help me weep! Jesus, give me Your heart! This world has worn on me. I have become callous and hard hearted. The ways of man have taught me "to be tough." Teach me to weep as You wept Lord. Help me weep over the lost, help me to weep over Your people, Israel. Do not let me go through my day as if this world is not on the fast track to hell. Break me Lord. I do not want to look back on my life and see a river of missed opportunities. Put a burning passion within me. Make me a person of passion. Help me weep with joy over Your goodness. Help me weep with sorrow over my sin and the sins of this world. Help me to rejoice with those who rejoice, and weep with those who weep.

Psalm 6:8-9

Depart from me, all you workers of iniquity; For the Lord has heard the voice of my weeping. The Lord has heard my supplication; The Lord will receive my prayer.

No matter what the world tries to tell me, no matter what this age tries to sell me, no matter what lies the enemy may whisper in my ear, I know that You hear me Lord. You have heard my every cry. You know the prayers that my lips have never even uttered. You hear my heart and know that pain I have held inside. And I know Lord that You will not always answer me in the way that I desire. For You are a good Father and You know when I need to learn patience and when I need to be chastened. You know my every need. Lord, You hold every tear I have ever wept in Your bottle. How dare I ever feel alone? I know that You are always with me. Thank You for being there for me. And thank You for saving me. I do not deserve Your great love, and yet You love me still. You are amazing, Father. May Your name ever be lifted high.

Psalm 7:1

O Lord my God, in You I put my trust; Save me from all those who persecute me; And deliver me.

Father, let me put my trust in You alone. Let me trust that if I love You with all my heart, and go where You tell me to go, that You will work all things to the good in my life. But Father, do not let me be deceived by Your great mercy. Never let me think that I have earned Your goodness and more so Lord, do not let me confuse your mercy on me with Your acceptance of my actions. Father, I plead with You, let me fall if You must. If I veer to the right or to the left, be swift with Your correction. If You find sin and iniquity in me, do whatever You must to bring me back to Your perfect will. I do not desire a smooth and easy ride. God, I desire to be Yours and Yours alone. Do what You must to bring me closer to You.

Psalm 7:11

God is a just judge,
And God is angry with the wicked every day.

Lord, as I look at the world around me, and see the error of their ways, it troubles me and it angers me. But Lord, if I, a sinner by nature, am angered, I can only imagine the fury You are withholding from a sinful world. Your ways are above my ways, Your ways are higher and greater. I do not fathom the depths of Your judgment, but I know that You are a good God and You are a just God. This world will get what is coming to it, but until then God, you mercifully relent. You do not desire to see the wicked perish. You desire for them to turn from their wicked ways and respond to Your everlasting gospel. I pray that they would turn God, but when You choose, the time will be right, and their judgement will be upon them. Thank You for your mercy towards me Lord. Thank You for saving me out of this wicked world and making me righteous through the blood of Your Son.

Psalm 8:1

How excellent is Your name in all the earth,
Who have set Your glory above the heavens!

Lord, it is so easy for me to look at things through an
earthly, worldly, naturalistic mindset. Help me keep things
in perspective. Remind me daily of just how great You are
and just how much You love me. Lord help my unbelief. I
treat my struggles like impassable mountains, but God, You
made the mountains! Even more Lord, You made the
heavens! The earth and moon and stars were made by the
word of Your voice! Let me never act like things are too big
for You to handle. And Lord, never let me fall into Satan's
lie that You wouldn't want to bless me with Your great
power. Lord, You esteem me greatly. You are mindful of
me. You have given me so very much. Father, never let me
forget how big You are and how loved I am.

Psalm 9:1

I will praise You, O Lord, with my whole heart; I will tell of
all Your marvelous works. I will be glad and rejoice in You;
I will sing praise to Your name, O Most High.

Oh my soul, sing praises to the LORD! Oh my God, You
are so good to me. Though I wander, You remain faithful.
Though I indulge the flesh, You woo me with Your Spirit.
God, You are both just and kind. Who am I to ever question
Your ways? God, You are teaching me to trust You. To
trust in Your goodness, Your kindness, Your fairness, and
Your amazing love for me. Though I have no offering
worthy to bring to You, You receive me anyway. Though I
am prone to wander, You come and You find me. Though I
am ungrateful for your chastisements, I do see them at work
in me. You are completing the good work You have begun
in me. You are purifying my heart and my mind. You are
making me more like Your son Jesus. Thank You Lord.
Thank You.

11

Psalm 9:10-11

*And those who know Your name will put their trust in You;
For You, Lord, have not forsaken those who seek You. Sing
praises to the Lord, who dwells in Zion! Declare His deeds
among the people.*

Lord, You have blessed me. You have never forsaken me
and You never will. You receive all who seek Your face.
Father, let my thanks be evident in my life. Prompt my heart
to sing Your praises everywhere I go. Let my light shine
before all men, that You might receive glory! Don't let me
just sing Your praises at church, but help me to sing from
the rooftops. Give me boldness to speak of Your great
blessings to everyone who will hear. Take away my pride.
Do not let me be self-conscious, but help me to be eternally
conscious. Keep my eyes on heaven and put a joy in my
heart that I cannot bear but to share it with this lost world.
Be glorified!

Psalm 9:13-14

*Have mercy on me, O Lord! Consider my trouble from those
who hate me, You who lift me up from the gates of death,
That I may tell of all Your praise In the gates of the
daughter of Zion. I will rejoice in Your salvation.*

Lord, let me never forget that You do not just bless me so
that I may be full, but You do so that You may be glorified.
That Your name be hallowed. Lord continue to bless me and
work in my life, that I may bless You. Hear all of my prayers,
that Your name be lifted up. Show Your great mercy to me,
so that I would rejoice in Your salvation and shout it from the
rooftops. Our God saves! You are amazing. Your mercies are
forever! Let these words always be on my lips. You are an
amazing God, and You are worthy of my praise. Lord
continue to bless me and work in my life, that I may bless
You. Hear all my prayers, that Your name be lifted up. Show
Your great mercy to me, so that I would rejoice in Your
salvation and shout it from the rooftops. Our God saves!

Psalm 9:18

For the needy shall not always be forgotten;
The expectation of the poor shall not perish forever.

Lord, it is sometimes hard to look around at the pain and
suffering in this world. I, in my finite understanding,
wonder, "how long, O Lord, will You allow this to
continue?" But I already know that the poor, the hungry,
and the persecuted will not always be that way. That, for the
time being, sin is in the world and mankind will suffer from
the results of sin, but very soon You will come for us! You
are coming quickly and You will put an end to sin and
suffering. You will wipe away every tear and create a new
heavens and a new earth. One where sin will reign no more
and we, Your children, will forever be at Your feet. I long
for that day Lord. I long to see Your glory and perfection.
But until that day, use me to accomplish Your will here on
the earth. Let Your kingdom come and Your will be done.
Amen Father, amen.

Psalm 10:1

Why do You stand afar off, O Lord?
Why do You hide in times of trouble?

LORD God, I do not understand Your ways, but I do try to
trust them. Your ways are above my ways and Your
thoughts are above my own. I cannot see the future as You
can. I cannot change the course of time, but I know that You
can and You do. Nothing is outside of Your hands. And so I
just have to trust You Lord. You allow the wicked to
remain, You allow suffering to continue, and You even
allow Your beloved children to suffer and die as martyrs,
but You have a plan that is beyond my comprehension.
Lord, I ask that You would just help me to trust You. Help
me trust You, even when I cannot fathom how You are
planning to work things to the good. Help me Lord. Your
servant needs You.

Psalm 10:16

The Lord is King forever and ever;
The nations have perished out of His land.

Lord, at times it seems like the enemy is winning. At times, I feel like You will tarry forever. Help my unbelief Lord. Never let me forget that no matter how things look, no matter how much the wicked prosper, no matter what happens to me, "The Lord is King forever and ever." You have everything in Your hands. You are in control. Nothing is outside of Your will for us. Lord, You do hear us. And You will bring all things to bear. Help us to trust that You are still King, You are on the throne, and no matter what happens, one day every knee will bow and every tongue will confess in the name of Your Son, Jesus.

Psalm 11:1

In the Lord I put my trust; How can you say to my soul,
"Flee as a bird to your mountain"?

Oh Lord my God, I do trust in You alone. You will never leave me nor forsake me. You loved me while I was still sinning against You, what could I ever do now that would make You not love me? Nothing! Your love for me is never ending and thus I will trust in You. You won't cast me away. In fact, You desire to build me up. You want to mold me into a righteous tool for Your using. Use me Lord to build Your kingdom. I am an empty canvas for You to draw upon. Have Your way in me Father. I know that the road ahead may be difficult. I know that sometimes it will even be painful. But I know that You are working in me and I trust You.

Psalm 11:7

For the Lord is righteous, He loves righteousness;
His countenance beholds the upright.

LORD God, let me be holy as You are Holy. You are Holy,
You are righteous, and You are true. You are never
changing and Your mercies endure forever and ever. God, I
desire to be holy as You are. Renew me by Your Spirit.
Keep me within Your love. Let my light shine into this dark
world and bring glory to Your awesome and powerful
name. Let my life be a testimony of Your great goodness
towards Your children. Father, I just want to glorify Your
great name through my actions. Let my heart be filled with
Your love and let it abound towards Your children. You are
so, so good Lord, my heart is Yours. Fill me and use me as
You choose. To You be all glory and honor. Amen.

Psalm 12:1

Help, Lord, for the godly man ceases!
For the faithful disappear from among the sons of men.

Lord, it can be so discouraging to see those who fall away.
Our friends and family who once burned strong for you now
glow dimly. But Lord, "a smoking flax You will not
quench". We know that You will not cast out even the
dimmest flame. Lord, restore our brother and sisters to You.
Keep them by Your side. And give us the strength to lift
them up in prayer daily. I know that Your desire to see their
restoration Lord. Bring them back to You. Lord, let Your
goodness bring them to repentance! Your mercies are
unending Father. I pray that You would show Yourself to
them, convict them of their ways, and bring them back to a
place of repentance.

Psalm 12:6

The words of the Lord are pure words, Like silver tried in a furnace of earth, Purified seven times.

While this world has betrayed me at times and my closest friends have let me down, Your Word has never failed Lord. Why do I continue to worry and trust in feeble things when I can simply look to Your Word? Help me to trust in Your Holy Word Father. I know that it is perfect and true. I know that it contains the fullness of Your Son, the fullness of grace and truth. Help me to rest in Your Word and help me to dive even deeper into the wonders of it. Let me be a sponge that soaks up the blessings contained in it. Let it be the first thought on my mind each morning and let me rest in its promises as I lay me down each night. Your Word will endure forever Father God. Thank You for Your Word.

Psalm 13:1

How long, O Lord? Will You forget me forever? How long will You hide Your face from me?

God, why do You sometimes feel so distant? Have I drifted again? Do You have a lesson in store for me? Are You trying to train me in some new thing? Lord, I do not like being apart from You. If You have some thing for me to learn through this, give me the strength I need to hold fast through this trial. But Father, if it is I who has drifted, correct me swiftly and get me back on to the narrow path that leads to Your righteous throne. Forgive me of my sins and reassure me that I have been thoroughly washed in the blood of Your Son Jesus. I know that You will never leave me, so help me find my way back when I wander.
I love You Lord. Lead me.

Psalm 13:5-6

But I have trusted in Your mercy; My heart shall rejoice in Your salvation. I will sing to the Lord, Because He has dealt bountifully with me.

Oh my Lord! You are so good to me. God, I am nothing that You should be concerned with me, yet You have made me of great value. No value that I could have earned. You have given me value. You sent Your Son to die for me. And it is so easy for me to become familiar and unenthusiastic about it, but it truly is a wonder above all wonders that You would come and die for a rebellious child like me. Never before would I have thought that I was worth dying for, but You did. Not only did You send Your Son to die for me, but You gave Your Spirit to live in me. Let me rest in this great peace, that Jesus died for a sinner like me, not because of my own worth, but because of the worth that You put on me. You have made me, and You will sustain me. I worship You my great King. Glory to You Father. Hallelujah.

Psalm 14:1

The fool has said in his heart, "There is no God." They are corrupt, They have done abominable works, There is none who does good.

Father, my heart breaks over those who are lost and do not know You. How has Your creation come to this? That people deny Your existence, yet the world around us testifies of who You are. God, unveil their eyes and save them from the lie that has been sold to them. Help them to see what they cannot see. Their hearts have become cold, Lord. Only You can bring them back. Help me to be sensitive to Your Holy Spirit and give me words to speak to them. I want to help them Father. Help me bring them back to You. Expose their evil ways so that they see what they are doing. Open their eyes to their own wickedness. And protect my heart that it does not grow cold because of their rejection of You. Keep me humble and keep me loving.
In Jesus' name I pray.

Psalm 14:2

The Lord looks down from heaven upon the children of men, To see if there are any who understand, who seek God.

Lord, I pray that when You look down upon Your children that You see me and that I am seeking You. Lord, I grow tired and become lazy at times. My faithfulness often varies. Yet in my heart I know that there is but one desire, to serve You and You alone! You are my King Lord Jesus. Command me where to go and what to do and I will do it. I only desire to serve You. By the power of Your Spirit inside of me, make me a fisher of men. I will follow You wherever You lead. Just overlook my sin, my ignorance, and my failures. Cast my sin as far as the east is from the west. Lord, I trust You. Lead the way my King, I will follow.

Psalm 15:1

A Psalm of David. Lord, who may abide in Your tabernacle? Who may dwell in Your holy hill?

Lord, I desire to abide in Your presence. I desire to dwell in Your house. Help me to be the kind of person whom You desire to dwell with. Help me to walk uprightly, live righteously, and have truth in my heart. Make me find no joy in the unrighteous. Give me the strength to keep my integrity, even if it comes at great cost. Plant my feet firmly in Your ways and lead me in the way of Your Son. Do not let anything have power over me. Help me to surrender my finances to You, my time, and my life. Lord, take my life as a living sacrifice, it is Yours. You have my all and my everything. I love You Abba Father. Thank You.

Psalm 16:1

Preserve me, O God, for in You I put my trust.

Father God, You are my only hope. I am unworthy and unable to fulfill the call that You have put on my life, but by Your grace I can carry on. No good thing dwells within me Lord, only You can preserve me. I trust in You Father. All of my hope and trust are in You. I am prone to look to myself for strength, but each time I do, You allow me to fail. For You have no desire for me to trust in myself. You lovingly let me stumble at times, only so that I will continue to look to You for strength. You humble me Lord and that is where I need to be, forever humbly before You. God You have saved me, You daily heal me, and You even uplift me. You are an amazing God. I pray that you remain the center of my life. Amen.

Psalm 16:2

O my soul, you have said to the Lord, "You are my Lord, My goodness is nothing apart from You."

Oh my Lord, truly my goodness is nothing apart from You. God, without You my good works would be for no other purpose than for selfish gain or personal satisfaction. I seek to please me first and others last, yet You have stepped in and You have changed me. You have given me a new heart, unlike the heart I once had. And though I still struggle with the sinful desires of my flesh, I know now what I ought to do. You are my God and my King and You alone I serve. Fill me afresh with Your Spirit Lord, that I may serve You righteously and with honor. Let my hands and my feet be consecrated into You. I give You all that I have and all that I am. Use Your servant Lord. I am willing.

Psalm 16:3

As for the saints who are on the earth, "They are the excellent ones, in whom is all my delight."

Lord God, You have made the mountains, the streams, the oceans, and the stars, and yet You delight in me. How can this be? How can You find delight in a person like me? It is Your grace God. You give to those who have not earned it. You love those who are not loveable. And You bestow Your riches on to Your children who so often rebel against You. It is only because You are such a great and loving God. Your ways are so far above my own. I pray Lord, that I can make You proud with what little I have to offer You. With every moment of my day, I pray that I can bring You joy and glory to Your name. Lord God, keep me from falling, so that I may glorify Your name. Help me to live for You because You gave Your Son for me.

Psalm 16:4

Their sorrows shall be multiplied who hasten after another god; Their drink offerings of blood I will not offer, Nor take up their names on my lips.

LORD God, I pray that You would take away the comforts of the wicked. Not as a punishment Lord, but so that they would become desperate and seek Your face. They do not believe that they need You, but they do. Lord, do Your will, but please bring more into Your flock. Let them who do not serve You be left desperate until they seek Your face. And until that day comes, help me to be free from their vices. Do not let me meddle with the ways of the wicked. Help me to live a holy and righteous life that brings honor to Your great name. I pray that I would be a worthy ambassador for Your great kingdom. Separate me from sin and use me to win more souls for Your kingdom. To You be all glory, honor, and praise Lord. You are amazing. Amen.

Psalm 16:5-6

O Lord, You are the portion of my inheritance and my cup; You maintain my lot. The lines have fallen to me in pleasant places; Yes, I have a good inheritance.

LORD God, I am not of this world. I am a sojourner and a pilgrim traveling through. No matter what happens to me during this earthly life, help me to remember that my inheritance is not here, but that it is with You. Everything in this world is going to burn, but Your kingdom is forever God. Help me turn my eyes from idols and false riches. Let me focus on the eternal ministry that You have designed me for. I want my life to be proposed to accomplish Your will because You are so very good to me. Lord, You heal me, You hold me, and You bless me beyond measure. Thank You for Your lovingkindness.

21

Psalm 16:7-8

I will bless the Lord who has given me counsel; My heart also instructs me in the night seasons. I have set the Lord always before me; Because He is at my right hand I shall not be moved.

Lord, I do not know where I would be today if You had not saved me. If I had been left alone to walk this life according to my own desires, I would have fallen long ago. But You saved me Lord. You reached down and You redirected my path; and You continue to guide me and counsel me, each day that I seek You. Lord, I pray that I will always seek Your counsel in all things. I know that You cannot be moved and cannot be defeated. Help me to walk the path You have set before me and trust in Your great strength. Father, I do not always understand Your ways, but I trust them. Lead me in the way everlasting. Forever and ever. Amen.

Psalm 16:11

You will show me the path of life; In Your presence is fullness of joy; At Your right hand are pleasures forevermore.

O God, how I long for Your presence; and how often I drift. Lord, You are a firm rock. You are immovable bedrock, but I drift like the tides. But Father, how I long for Your presence. To hear Your voice, to see Your face, to feel Your arms around me. Lord, I am continually desperate for You. Do not forsake me. I am utterly unworthy of Your love, yet Your grace abounds in my life. I am a testimony of man's unfaithfulness and Your great faithfulness. You do seek me out and find me when I stray. You do comfort me when I have fallen. And in Your presence I experience fullness of joy. Oh how I long for the day when I will forever be in Your presence. The pains and sorrows of this world long gone and Your glory shining forevermore. Lord, show me the path of life that leads to Your throne. Keep me forever by Your side. Amen.

Psalm 17:1

Hear a just cause, O Lord, Attend to my cry; Give ear to my prayer which is not from deceitful lips.

Lord, let me pray with confidence as David prayed. God, I do not want my sin to separate me from Your perfect will. If there is a hint of rebellion in me, search it out and make it known to me. Test my heart and show me if I am found lacking. God, I want nothing in my life that would take away from the great work You desire to do in me. Give me a great confidence in Your salvation. Remind me daily that You, and You alone, have paid the price for me. You have freed me from sin, now let me walk boldly in that freedom. I am Yours Father. Save me.

Psalm 17:5

Uphold my steps in Your paths, That my footsteps may not slip.

My great Father in heaven, hallowed be Thy name. And Lord God over all creation, lead me not into temptation, that Your name might be hallowed. God, I appeal to You, to Your goodness, Your mercies, and the promises of Your Word. Keep me! Keep me from falling so that my life does not tarnish Your great name. Keep me from folly, that others would not blaspheme Your name. Father, keep me from returning to that sin which I am so easily stumbled by. God, I appeal to You to protect me from my foolish self and this body of flesh that I must endure until the end. Until that Day, when You give me a glorious body like Your Son's, please keep me from falling. Lord, the enemy's stumbling blocks are nothing as long as I keep my eyes on You. Keep me Lord. Keep me.

Psalm 17:15

As for me, I will see Your face in righteousness;
I shall be satisfied when I awake in Your likeness.

Lord Jesus, how glorious it will be when I awake in Your likeness. Conform me into Your image. Complete the good work which You have started in and keep me from falling back into my old ways. When people saw You, they saw the Father, and when people see me, I want them to see You at work in me. Lord, help me to love others the way You loved them. Let me live a life of sacrificial love. Give me the strength to put others before myself. Help make me low so that You may be lifted higher. Lord, let me never take the glory for the work that You are doing in me. Let all honor, and glory, and praise go to Your great name.

Psalm 18:1-2

I will love You, O Lord, my strength.

Lord, help me quit looking to my own strength and allow me to come into total submission to Your great will. Father, I am so prone to ask for strength to face things, when ultimately You may be trying to have me find no strength in myself and find all my strength in You. Oh, woe to the times that I pray for strength when You just want me to be broken. Your will be done Father! Let me hand over my anxieties and my problems to You and let me let go of my struggles! Help me to trust in Your great strength and Your strength alone. You are my rock! You are my deliverer! Help me not trust in me, but in You alone.

24

Psalm 18:6

In my distress I called upon the Lord, And cried out to my God; He heard my voice from His temple, And my cry came before Him, even to His ears.

Oh how wonderful it is to be heard by the Lord of Hosts! Lord, You hear my every cry and You catch my every tear. You know all that I am and You love me still. LORD God, I ask that You would protect me from the lies of the evil one. Do not let me be tricked into thinking that You do not hear me. For I know that when I cry out to You, You hear me and You answer. Help me to trust in Your ways. Though You often do not give me what I ask for, You always give me what I need. You are truly a good, good Father and know how to give good gifts to Your children. Thank You for blessing me so much with the gifts that You have given me. I know that You have a plan for me. Help me to walk in that plan. And Lord, today again I cry out to You. Hear Your child and answer. I want to feel Your presence.

Psalm 18:33

He makes my feet like the feet of deer, And sets me on my high places.

Lord God Almighty, make me like the Ibex! Make me like the mountain goat! Teach me to climb to the highest of heights and let this world be in awe of what can be done by those who trust in You. I want to have a supernatural faith. I want to live like no one else, wholly trusting in Your provision and Your power. Use me to do Your will oh God. Use me to accomplish Your will here on this earth. Let all who see me, see He who is in me. Let me shine ever so bright and You receive the glory. Let me live for You God.

Psalm 19:1-2

The heavens declare the glory of God; And the firmament shows His handiwork. Day unto day utters speech, And night unto night reveals knowledge.

LORD God, we cry out to You, let this world see Your hand in Your creation. Let it testify of who You are. God, soften their hard hearts and have them put their trust in You. Lord, Your works are clearly seen. The evidence of Your greatness goes throughout the whole earth. God, they are foolish, those who deny You. Please Lord, unveil their eyes. Let Your light shine upon them and turn them away from the darkness which they love. We cannot reach them if You do not go out before us. Lead the way Lord and soften the sinners' hearts. We want to see many come to salvation. Help us to serve You Lord. To You be all glory and honor and praise. Hallelujah, amen.

Psalm 19:7

The law of the Lord is perfect, converting the soul; The testimony of the Lord is sure, making wise the simple;

LORD God, keep me in Your Word daily. Have it wash me and purify me. Father, I ask that You keep me humble. Show me your ways Lord and teach me through Your Word. Daily draw me towards You and daily remind me of who I am in Christ. Let me trust in Your Word and not in the lies of the enemy. Do not let Satan have a place in my heart or mind. I pray that Your Word would surround me and fill me. That through Your Word I would be made more and more like Your Son Jesus. Father God, I want to see You. Show me Yourself daily through Your Word. Keep me in Your Word. Bless me by Your Word.

Psalm 19:9

The fear of the Lord is clean, enduring forever; The judgments of the Lord are true and righteous altogether. More to be desired are they than gold, Yea, than much fine gold; Sweeter also than honey and the honeycomb.

Lord, in a world full of lies, You speak truth. Truth is found in Your Son Jesus and in Your Word. You have given us all things that we could ever need in this life and all things that we need to pursue godliness, yet we often find ourselves taking matters into our own hands. We try to solve things our ways. Lord, let me not wander from the path You have set me on. Your ways are not only right, but they are good.
Lord, Your Word is not a burden to me, it is a great comfort. I rest in Your truth. I desire to follow Your ways because I know that they are good. Bless me Lord, bless me with Your everlasting goodness. Amen.

Psalm 19:14

Let the words of my mouth and the meditation of my heart Be acceptable in Your sight, O Lord, my strength and my Redeemer.

Holy Spirit, convict me of my sins and transgressions if I am in error. I do not want to be ignorantly disobeying Your perfect will. Be quick to correct me and keep me on Your righteous path. I desire to be blameless before Your eyes. I desire to bring glory to Your name with my life. Lord, I do not care if I am right among men, I only care to be acceptable in Your sight. Lead me, guide me, push me, and prod me. Do whatever it takes to make me the person You want me to be.
O Lord, You are my strength. You are my Redeemer.

Psalm 20:3

May He remember all your offerings,
And accept your burnt sacrifice.

Lord, if I had anything worth giving, I would give it all to You. Whatever I have, I want You to have it. Take my possessions, take my life, take my thoughts. I give them all to You Lord. Most of all, I pray that You receive the offering of my obedience. There is not a thing I own that You would honor more than my simple obedience to You. I pray Lord, that my life is acceptable before Your eyes. Help me to flee from sin and help me to run to help those in need. Let me not repay evil for evil, but help me to bless those who curse me and turn the other cheek when I am abused. I want my life to bring honor to Your name. Many who call on Your name will choose to live for themselves, but I want to live for You alone. Here I am Lord, send me.

Psalm 20:4

May He grant you according to your heart's desire,
And fulfill all your purpose.

Lord, if I pray to You, I hope that I only pray about that which You desire me to pray about. And Lord, if You grant me the desires of my heart, I pray that my heart is aligned with You perfect will. Father God, not my will, but Thy will be done. I do not want anything for myself. I want less of me and more of You. Let my prayers be Your prayers Father. Let my heart be Your heart. I want to see Your will done here in earth as it is in heaven. Who am I that the Lord of the universe should listen to me? I am nobody of significance, yet You hear me still! You hear my every prayer and You answer when I call. Great are You Lord and great are Your works in all the earth! I worship You. Amen.

Psalm 20:7
Some trust in chariots, and some in horses;
But we will remember the name of the Lord our God.

Father, I do not want to trust in anything, or anyone, but
You alone. Please, reveal to me if I am trusting in anything
that is not You alone. I do not want to trust in schemes,
plans, procedures, paychecks, insurances, assurances of
man, or even my own body. Let me look to You for all my
strength because You never fail. It is impossible for You,
the LORD, to ever fail! Help me to remember this! If I trust
in anything, aside from You, I will be let down, but if I trust
in You alone, I can rest assured that all things will work to
the good in my life. Thank You Father for being so loving
and understanding. Praise You for Your Son and Your
Spirit. Hallelujah.

Psalm 21:6
For You have made him most blessed forever;
You have made him exceedingly glad with Your presence.

Oh God, there is nothing on the earth, nor in the heavens
above, nor in the depths below, nor any created thing, that I
desire more than Your presence. Father, to hear Your voice
brings tears to my eyes and sends waves of joy throughout
my soul. Who am I that You would speak to me? I am
beyond unworthy, yet You shine Your grace upon me. I
hunger for Your presence Lord. While this world causes me
to drift away, I soon sense the distance I have created, and
so I come running back to You. I want to live forever in
Your arms. I want to lay my head upon Your chest. As You
have promised, never leave me nor forsake me Lord! I live
for You and You alone. Keep me close by Your side and let
me feel Your presence today more than ever before.

Psalm 21:13
Be exalted, O LORD, in Your own strength!
We will sing and praise Your power.

Father, Your power is unending and Your glory is outstanding. You are the creator God. You are the Lord of heaven and earth. You are my Redeemer! You are my Mighty Counselor! You are my friend. I pray that in my house Your name will forever be lifted high. Let me sing honor, and glory, and praise to You, all the days of my life. Father God, move with power in my town. Let all the people see that You are the God of miracles. You restore the sinner and heals the brokenhearted. You mend what no man could mend and fix what no man could fix. Your power is without end and still You think of me. Thank You Father for remembering Your children. We love You Lord and we worship You.

Psalm 22:1
My God, My God, why have You forsaken Me? Why are You
so far from helping Me, And from the words of My groaning?

Oh Lord, who am I that You would forsake Your Son for me? Your actions speak the truth, I am beloved in Your sight. You gave it all, just so that I could be reconciled to You. My worth is not in my own self, but in the worth You placed on me when You purchased me by the blood of Your Son. You have given me grace freely, but at the greatest of cost. You laid down His life, in order to save mine. LORD God, help me to live the life of one whom has been set free. For I am free indeed. And all because your forsook Your Son. Thank You Lord! Forever I will praise You for what You have done for me. You are amazing and worthy of all praise. Hallelujah Father thank You for Your amazing grace!

Psalm 22:16

For dogs have surrounded Me; The congregation of the wicked has enclosed Me. They pierced My hands and My feet;

Lord God, You knew the end of the story before it began! God, You are all knowing and all powerful and yet You sent Your beloved Son Jesus to save a sinner like me. God, I am in awe of You! You are so amazing and so compassionate, I can hardly find words that describe You. Thank You Father! Thank You Jesus for dying for me. Even when You knew that I would turn from You and sin against You, You already planned to save me. What great love You have for me! My heart overflows with gratitude. You loved me while I was unlovable and You love me still. Help me to rest in Your great love. Help me respect Your great love. Let me live my life in a way that honors You, because You considered my life worth dying for. Holy Spirit, guide me and protect me every day. Keep me on the path that honors the Father. Amen.

Psalm 23:1-3

The LORD is my shepherd; I shall not want. He makes me to lie down in green pastures; He leads me beside the still waters. He restores my soul; He leads me in the paths of righteousness For His name's sake.

Lord God, I want to lift Your name high and bring You praise in all that I do. Thank You Yahweh God that You provide for me, always, to the glory of Your great name! Thank You that You supply all my needs and bring me to a place of comfort and rest. All for Your great name's sake! Thank You Jesus that You have paid the price for my soul. You have bought me with Your precious blood and have brought me from death into life. All for the glory and praise of Your great name! Oh, thank You Holy Spirit! Continue always to guide me and lead me down the path of righteousness. Convict me of any sin or iniquity that is within me and lead me down Your righteous path. Let me live a righteous and holy life, all to glorify Your great name! Let all that I do bring glory, and honor, and praise to You and Your holy name.

32

Psalm 23:4

Yea, though I walk through the valley of the shadow of death, I will fear no evil; For You are with me; Your rod and Your staff, they comfort me.

Lord let Your presence always bring comfort to me. Help me to feel Your presence when the trials of this life begin to drag me down. Father God, You are almighty and powerful, nothing can stop You, and nothing can hinder You. Let me never forget that You are on my side. I desire to feel Your great power at work in my life. Lord, let me not despise Your correction or Your direction. Let me find peace in Your guiding. Lord, I know that because I am Your child, You will chasten me when needed and I beg You to spare nothing. I want you to purge me of anything that would keep me from the fullness of Your working presence in my life. Let me not fear Your chastening but let me find comfort in knowing that You love me enough to correct me. I am Yours Lord God. Save me.

Psalm 23:6

Surely goodness and mercy shall follow me All the days of my life; And I will dwell in the house of the LORD Forever.

Lord, let my heart's desire be to dwell in Your presence. Lord You are welcome here in my life, in my heart, and in my soul. Come like a rushing wind and flood my surroundings. Let my heart desire nothing more than to be in Your presence. Oh God, I long for Your presence in my life. Let me feel You as You are near to me. Let me meditate upon Your never-ending goodness Lord. Oh, how I long to be with You in eternity. Comfort me Holy Spirit and keep me by Your side until the Father calls me home.

Psalm 24:3-4

Who may ascend into the hill of the LORD? Or who may stand in His holy place? He who has clean hands and a pure heart, Who has not lifted up his soul to an idol, Nor sworn deceitfully.

Oh LORD! I desire to ascend Your holy hill! I desire to stand in Your presence! Cleanse me! Father, wash me of my sins and make me a vessel totally consecrated unto You! Lord, this world desires to taint me with sin. It wants to lure me away from You. God look into my heart and convict me by Your Holy Spirit if there is anything that displeases You within me. Lord I want my heart to be pure before You. Cleanse me, wash me, and protect me Lord! Do not let me lift my soul to any idol. Let me put no faith in persons or in things, but in You alone! God, do not let me create a graven image, do not let me believe in a God of my own making. Make me believe in You alone, as You have revealed Yourself to me in Your holy Word! Thank You for Your Word Father. Thank You for Your work in my life. Hold me close Abba. I need You.

Psalm 24:6

This is Jacob, the generation of those who seek Him, Who seek Your face.

Oh God let us be a generation that seeks the face of the God of Jacob! Lord, You wrestled with Jacob and You came to Moses. These men came to see You as face to face. Lord, let this generation be a generation that seeks You face to face. Lord, I pray that we would break our hearts and bend our knees and come before You in all humility. Set a fire within our hearts that longs for nothing except revival fire. Lord God, we want to see You move with power. Let Your Church feel Your presence. Father, we long for You. Our hearts cry out to You. Come and be our God. Let us never turn our eyes to another created thing. You alone are the desire of our hearts God. Rule and reign within us. We long for You Father. We long for You.

Psalm 24:7

Lift up your heads, O you gates! And be lifted up, you everlasting doors! And the King of glory shall come in.

Dearest Lord, humbly I come before You on behalf of the ones that I love. Father it often appears as if they have blinders on their eyes, plugs in their ears, and bars over their hearts. I speak to them about Your goodness and yet the words seem to bounce right off of them. Lord God, only Your Holy Spirit can soften the heart of sinful man. I pray that You would do a work in them Lord. God I pray that they would open the gates to their heart and let You, the King of Glory, come inside. I pray that they would make You the King of their hearts. For You are a King, mighty and powerful, sovereign, righteous, and true. And most of all Father, You are good. You are so, so, good. Lord God, let my friends and family know Your goodness. Let them open up to You and let You come in. Amen.

Psalm 25:4-5

Show me Your ways, O LORD; Teach me Your paths. Lead me in Your truth and teach me, For You are the God of my salvation; On You I wait all the day.

God, let me not care what others think and let my heart be given over to Your truth. Father I do not want to live in any way that is opposed to Your perfect will for my life. Show me what You want of me Lord and it is Yours. I want to give you ALL that I have. Every last ounce of my strength, every last second of my day, it is Yours to keep. God, how would I have ever known Your ways if You had not taught them to me. Continue to teach me Father. Guide me down the path that brings glory and honor to Your name. Let Your name be hallowed by the life that I live. For You are my God! And I love You deeply! With all of my heart Lord. Take it, it is Yours and Yours alone. Amen

Psalm 25:6-7

Remember, O LORD, Your tender mercies and Your loving kindnesses, For they are from of old. Do not remember the sins of my youth, nor my transgressions; According to Your mercy remember me, For Your goodness' sake, O LORD.

Oh LORD, You overwhelm me with Your goodness. I will never be able to earn Your favor because You give it to me freely and undeserved. Lord, be honored for Your mercies and longsuffering. You have not only forgiven my sins, but You have forgotten them. And not because I am good, but because You are so good! Oh Jesus, that You would die for a rebel like me! Thank You. Thank You Lord. Let my life be a song of praise to You. Let all that I do bring glory to Your great name. Let the name of our God be greatly praised! Thank You Lord, thank You.

Psalm 26:2
Examine me, O LORD, and prove me;
Try my mind and my heart.

Lord God, let me walk with the confidence of Your servant David. Father, I desire that each time I come before You, that I can say with confidence that I have been putting my trust in You alone. That I have walked in Your truth. And that I have not kept company with the wicked. Lord, I want every blessing that You would have for me and I want to be a clean and suitable dwelling place for Your Holy Spirit. Give me a heart like David's. Break my heart for what breaks Yours. Let me love what You love. Abba Father, I want to make You proud. Let my life bring joy to Your heart. Give me strength Lord, apart from You I am nothing.

Psalm 26:8
LORD, I have loved the habitation of Your house,
And the place where Your glory dwells.

Lord God, I pray for Your Church. The Bride of Christ. Lord, though I know that the gates of hell shall not prevail against her, some days it appears so. So much wickedness has crept in Father. Many preach Christ for selfish gain, others water down Your gospel to the point where I no longer know if what they preach even has saving power. Yet Your Church cannot fail. She is blood bought and blood washed. Lord God, I pray now for my church. Lord, the fellowship of believers that You have called me to. I pray that Your presence is powerfully within our midst. I pray that You give us all a zeal for Your house. That like Your Son, zeal for Your house would eat us up. I pray that You give us great unity and oneness of spirit. Lord, let our church burn hot for You. Spark a revival within our midst and let Your kingdom come, on earth as it is in heaven.

Psalm 27:11
Teach me Your way, O LORD,
And lead me in a smooth path, because of my enemies.

Father, teach me Your ways. Continue to complete the work
that You have started in me. Father God, help me to be
submissive to Your perfect will and listening for Your
guidance so that You will not have to correct me along the
way. Lord, if I wander from the path, correct me swiftly. Do
not let me wander far, so that the correction must be great.
Deal promptly with me. But Lord, You know best and I do
not want to stand in the way of the work You desire in me,
so let Your will be done. God, I just pray that for Your
name's sake that You keep me walking smoothly down
Your path, so that the scoffers will have no reason, from
me, to doubt in Your great name. Lord, give me ears that
are ready to hear, and a heart that is ready to listen. I am
Yours Abba. Amen.

Psalm 27:14
Wait on the LORD; Be of good courage, And He shall
strengthen your heart; Wait, I say, on the LORD!

Lord I can be so impatient at times. Father, forgive me for
trying to have You work on my schedule. Teach me to have
patience and to wait upon the moving of Your Holy Spirit.
Give me the strength and courage that I need. God, I need to
trust in Your wisdom. You work all things to the good in
my life. Help me to just keep loving You and listening to
Your instructions. I don't want to move on without You.
Again Father, give me patience. Give me peace in troubled
times. And help me to trust in the promises of Your Word.

Psalm 27:4

One thing I have desired of the LORD, That will I seek: That I may dwell in the house of the LORD All the days of my life, To behold the beauty of the LORD, And to inquire in His temple.

Oh Lord, keep my eyes always on the heavens. My flesh is drawn to the things of this earth, but I want to live a life that glorifies You alone. And I want to be in Your presence. Lord, You do not keep company with the wicked, so cleanse me Father. Wash me with the blood of Your Son and allow me to enter into Your presence. God, I want to behold Your beauty. I want the presence of Your Holy Spirit to be the thing that draws me in this world, not the things of the flesh. Lord, take hold of my heart, draw me to You. Keep me close by Your side so that I don't stumble and fall. Lord, there is no place that I'd rather be, than here in the presence of Your great love. Hallelujah Father! I love You.

Psalm 27:7-8

Hear, O LORD, when I cry with my voice! Have mercy also upon me, and answer me. When You said, "Seek My face," My heart said to You, "Your face, LORD, I will seek."

Father God You are amazing! You bless me and bless me! Lord, You are merciful and compassionate. I would have given up on me a long time ago, but You were longsuffering with me. Jesus, You came and died for me while I was still rejecting You. And now I am Yours Lord. Lord, You say, "seek My face," and God, I will seek You with all of my heart! You are my heart's desire. I long for Your presence, I long for Your guidance, God I wait quietly here to hear Your voice. Speak to me Lord! Your servant is here. Pick me, I will go where You ask. Let me glorify Your name, here on earth as it is in heaven. Let my life hallow the name of Jesus. Guide me Father, Your servant is listening.

Psalm 28:1

To You I will cry, O LORD my Rock: Do not be silent to me,
Lest, if You are silent to me, I become like those who go
down to the pit.

Lord, I pray for Your great name's sake that You hear my
prayers and You answer them Father. Lord, with faith I ask
You to glorify and hallow Your great name through the
answering of my prayer. Let those who are against You see
Your mighty hand at work. Lord, let my prayers only be
those things that would bring glory to You. I desire for You
to be known as Yahweh Jireh, the God Who provides and
Yahweh Rapha, the God Who heals! You are the great Lord
over all creation, the Maker of the heavens and the earth!
Lord, hear my prayers, answer them, and make Your great
power be known to all mankind! I pray this Father, in the
name of Your holy Son, Jesus.

Psalm 28:9

Save Your people, And bless Your inheritance;
Shepherd them also, And bear them up forever.

Father God, I need You so very much! Lord, thank You,
praise You Father, for saving a person like me. Lord I never
did deserve Your great mercy and grace, and I never will.
But Father, now that You have saved me, now that You
have reached down and plucked me out of the mire, God I
ask that You would shepherd me. And I ask that You would
transform my heart so that I would not reject Your leading.
Lord, both Your correcting rod and Your guiding staff, they
comfort me. Just to know that You are near gives me a
peace that cannot be described. Father, thank You again for
your mercies. Thank You for your grace. Keep me ever
mindful of all the great things You have done for me. I don't
want a moment to go by where I forget about Your great
sacrifice. Thank You Father. Thank You.

Psalm 29:1-2
Give unto the LORD, O you mighty ones,
Give unto the LORD glory and strength.

Lord God, take all that I am. Have Your way in me and let
the deeds of my life be a sweet aroma to You. Father, help
me to live in holiness, not for my sake God, but for the
glory and hallowing of Your great name. Lord, let this
world see the miracle of a transformed life and let all glory
be pointed back at You. Lord Jesus, only You could have
saved a sinner like me. Holy Spirit, let me make this bodily
temple a clean and holy place for You to abide. Father, keep
me from sin so that I bring glory to You in my life. Help my
whole life to be a song of praise unto You. God, You blow
my mind day after day. Keep me in awe of Your greatness
and submitted to Your perfect law. Have it convert my soul.
Have Your way in me today Father. Always and forever.
Amen.

Psalm 29:4
The voice of the LORD is powerful;
The voice of the LORD is full of majesty.

Oh LORD God Almighty, let me hear Your voice! Oh God,
Your voice is lovely. Your voice is powerful. Your voice is
comforting. Your voice is commanding. Lord, at the sound
of Your voice, You bring me to tears. Tears of joy and tears
of unworthiness. Your voice pierces to the depths of my
soul. Hearing You speak overwhelms me and shakes me to
my core. But Oh God, speak again! Lord, I long to hear
from You each day. I wait upon You Lord, direct Your
servant and give me strength. Oh how I love to hear from
You. With the same voice that You spoke the heavens and
earth into existence You whisper in my ear a song of love.
Oh God, how I love Your voice. Speak Lord, Your servant
hears. Speak Lord, Your servant is listening.

Psalm 30:2
O LORD my God, I cried out to You, And You healed me.

Father, before I knew You my life was filled with brokenness. I was broken on the inside and outwardly I longed for satisfaction from all the wrong places. I was lost Father. So lost that I did not know the way back. Yet in my wandering and in my folly, I cried out to You. In Your kindness and longsuffering, You let me wander. You knew my stubborn heart. You knew I would not cry out until my need was great. My broken life became more shattered. The place in which I wandered became even darker. Yet in my darkest hour, broken and hurting, I cried out to You, and You answered my cry, and You healed me. God, You have healed me and You have blessed me. You healed my wounds and You have given me a crown. I am unworthy of Your goodness God and I long for the day when I can cast that crown before Your feet. Blessed be the Name of the Lord of Hosts. All glory and honor and praise be Yours forever and ever, amen.

Psalm 30:4-5
Sing praise to the LORD, you saints of His, And give thanks at the remembrance of His holy name. For His anger is but for a moment, His favor is for life; Weeping may endure for a night, But joy comes in the morning.

Lord, every day I need You to restore my vision of eternity. Daily I quickly lose focus on eternal things and the temporal things of this world distract me from Your plans and Your will. Lord, let me not fear Your temporary chastisements and remember that You are preparing me for eternity. God, never let the pains and struggles of this life overshadow the joy that is to come. Lord, I do not want to look back on my life and see a life lived with only this world in mind. God, I want to look back and see that I lived continually with Your eternal will in mind. Help me to have an eternal mindset. Help me to weigh my decisions based on eternal consequences and not earthly ones. And again Father, let no present pains ever take my mind off of the joy that is to come. Thank You Father. Amen.

Psalm 31:1

In You, O LORD, I put my trust; Let me never be ashamed;
Deliver me in Your righteousness.

Oh Lord, for Your name's sake, protect me, lead me, and
guide me. Lord keep me from falling, not just for my sake,
but for Your name's sake. Lord, I want to be a testimony to
this world of Your goodness. God, I want people to see how
good You are and how great You save! Do not let me be put
to shame, for that would bring shame to You! Let me
represent Christ with honor and dignity. Let me bring glory
to Him through my life. Father, help me to lead a life of
good works that all point back to You. I want to see You
lifted high Lord. Show Yourself strong in me.

Psalm 31:5

Into Your hand I commit my spirit; You have redeemed me,
O LORD God of truth.

Father in heaven, You have redeemed me from a life of sin.
You took out my selfish heart of stone and gave me one like
Your own. It feels so good to be made new. God, I give You
my all and my everything. Take my often rebellious spirit
and change it to be more like Your Holy Spirit. Refresh and
renew me daily to be a vessel of Your goodness. I place my
life into Your hands. All I desire is to be used by You for
Your glory Father God. Let this redeemed tool be used by
You to accomplish Your works here on the earth. Oh God
of truth, let Your Word be on my lips and Your Spirit in my
heart. Help me to submit to Your perfect will and let my life
bring You all honor and glory and praise. Praise You Lord.

Psalm 31:19

Oh, how great is Your goodness, Which You have laid up for those who fear You, Which You have prepared for those who trust in You In the presence of the sons of men!

Lord Jesus, thank You so much for saving me. You came for me when I was still in rebellion against You. Lord, thank You for Your great gift. And Lord, I do not just want to settle for Your gift of salvation, Lord I want all the goodness that You would have for me. Help me to fear You and trust You so that I can receive all that You would give. Create a clean vessel out of me that is prepared to be used for whatever You will. Let those around me see the good work that You have started in me and I pray Lord that I never stand in Your way of completing it. Have Your way in me Lord. Take all of me. Amen.

Psalm 32:1

*Blessed is he whose transgression is forgiven,
Whose sin is covered.*

Yes Lord, there is no other word for those whom have been forgiven by You, we are blessed. It is not of works that we have done, nor a plan that we have made, but by Your mercy and grace You have blessed us. And so my heart cries out to You Lord, thank You. Thank You for blessing me so. Lord it is by Your mercy alone that I am forgiven and it is by Your grace alone that You have called me Your child. You are beyond good to me God. Even when I stumble, even when I fall, You are there blessing me. Words cannot express the gratitude that I have towards You. Nor can words truly describe the love that You have shown towards me. Thank You Father for Your goodness, thank You for Your mercies, and thank You for Your Son.

Psalm 32:3-4

When I kept silent, my bones grew old. Through my groaning all the day long. For day and night Your hand was heavy upon me; My vitality was turned into the drought of summer.

LORD God, I cannot keep silent any longer. I cannot hide from the things which You have shown me. I cannot run Lord, where else can I go? Lord, to ignore You only brings me pain and suffering. If I try to numb it or become calloused, You give me no rest. Lord, Your hand is heavy upon me. I know what You desire from me. I know what my sacrifice ought to be. Lord Jesus, here I am. All of me. Everything. Completely. God, I am Yours. Forever and always. Forgive my stubbornness Lord. Forgive my selfishness. I want to be Yours, always and forever. You are my Lord and my King. Use me as You desire. Let me truly be expendable for You. My life is in Your hands Lord. I am Yours. Moment by moment and day by day, I am Yours.

Psalm 32:5

I acknowledged my sin to You, And my iniquity I have not hidden. I said, "I will confess my transgressions to the LORD" And You forgave the iniquity of my sin.

Here I am God! You see me. You know me. Nothing is hidden from before Your eyes. God, I am a sinner. I always have been and I apparently will always be prone to be. My flesh cries out Lord. It has no desire to be put under subjection, but You have given me Your Spirit Lord and He guides me and comforts me. I know what I ought to do, yet so often I fail. I fail to do the things that I know I should. I even stumble and do the things that I clearly know I should not. How is it that You still forgive me so freely? How is it that You have not forsaken me yet? God, whom am I that You should love me? You are YHWH God! You are the Lord! I am speechless Lord. You give and You give and all we ever seem to do is take. Your mercies are mind blowing Father. Your love is so perfect and pure. Your children are blessed beyond comprehension. God, thank You for being so loving. Help us to live for You. Help us make You proud. Help me to be faithful Father. Help me to live for You. God, You are good.   .

Psalm 32:6

For this cause everyone who is godly shall pray to You In a time when You may be found; Surely in a flood of great waters They shall not come near him.

Lord, with all of Your promises, all of Your direction, and all of the testimonies of Your Word, why do we not pray like we ought to? What has happened to the midweek prayer meeting? Where have the full nights of prayer gone? Where is the praying saint of old? Do Your people not know that You are found in prayer? That You hear our intercessions and are heard by us wherever we cry? Have they never heard the still small voice that graciously replies in times often unexpected. That You condescend and speak with sinful man. You utter a single word in our ear and it shakes us to our core. With but a whisper You can turn the prayer's world upside down and manifest Your glory. Lord God, help us to pray to You. Help us to seek Your face. Father, in a time when the flood waters are rising, help us to call out on Your name for deliverance. You have never forsaken us and You will not forsake us now. Lord, teach us to pray.

Psalm 32:7

You are my hiding place; You shall preserve me from trouble; You shall surround me with songs of deliverance.

Oh Lord, my God, You are my hiding place. You are the source of power in which I trust. And Lord, You are the steady Rock on which I stand. When troubles come, I flee to You. When darkness surrounds me, I cling to Your great light. So often I want You to remove all of my troubles, but You have wisely preserved me through them. Trial by trial I grow in Your Word and Your ways. You have taught me that Your Word never fails. My memory and obedience may sometimes falter, but Your Truth remains steadfast. This world does not know the peace that You bring. When the enemy attacks, I am not only surrounded by Your loving arms, but You play a song for me. You comfort me with great comforts. You remind me of Your majesty. You prepare a table for me before my enemies and You break bread with me there. O Lord, my God, You are my hiding place.

Psalm 32:8
I will instruct you and teach you in the way you should go;
I will guide you with My eye.

Gracious Father God, I come to You seeking Your guidance
and direction. Lord, I do not desire to walk down any path
that You have not set before me. Help me to be patient and
willing to wait on You. Do not let me act in haste. Lord
Jesus, You lead the way and I will follow. I want to follow
you all of my days. Guide me Lord. Give me Your peace
that surpasses understanding so that I may know that I am
walking in accordance with Your will. I only want to bring
honor and glory to You and Your great name. Thank You
for hearing my prayers Father and thank you Jesus for
making the way. Amen.

Psalm 32:9
Do not be like the horse or like the mule, Which have no
understanding, Which must be harnessed with bit and
bridle, Else they will not come near you.

Father, thank You for being so longsuffering towards me.
Lord, regardless of Your continual warnings, I am often a
mule at heart! I can be so stubborn. I can be very rebellious.
I kick and I claw. Lord, You do not desire to keep me under
bit and bridle, but I am thankful that You do at times.
Father, restrain me when I am foolish. Do not let me wander
farther than I must. My feet ache in pain from kicking at
Your goads. You are so patient, Lord! Bless You! Praise
You! What a patient Father You are! Lord God, lead me in
Your ways and give me understanding. Help me to trust
You and stay on Your path. Let Your Holy Word lead me
and guide me. Help me to surrender to the moving of Your
Spirit. Give me a tender heart and attentive ears to hear the
wishes of my Master. Let me be fit for Your use and always
ready and by Your side. Lord, thank You for Your
graciousness. You are an amazing God.

Psalm 33:1

Rejoice in the LORD, O you righteous!
For praise from the upright is beautiful.

Oh great and merciful Father in heaven, You are good! Lord
God, hear my praise! Forgive me that I often only come to
You with needs, for now I just desire to praise You. Let my
lips sing You praises in the morning and in the afternoon.
Let my hands be lifted high to You before I lay down to
sleep. Lord, I pray that my whole life is like a sweet song to
You. Let my mouth, my hands, and my feet all be used to
bring You praise. For You are worthy Lord, worthy of all
my praise. I pray that my worship is acceptable before Your
eyes. Be blessed Father by the songs of Your child. I lift
them up to You. Hallelujah to my great God!

Psalm 33:18

Behold, the eye of the LORD is on those who fear Him,
On those who hope in His mercy,

Oh Lord, my hope is in You alone. If there is one thing that
each passing day teaches me, it is that I am a sinner in need
of a Savior. How my heart so quickly drifts, I do not know.
In the morning I seek you and by the evening I seek me.
Help me to forever keep my eyes upon You Lord. Help me
to remember the warnings in Your Word. Hide Your Word
in my heart Father. Bring reminders to my ears throughout
the day. Help me to walk on Your path and to turn neither to
the left nor to the right. I want to walk on the straight and
narrow. I want to stay on Your path for me. Be my light and
be my guide. Be my all in all. Oh Lord, You're beautiful.
Let Your face be all I seek.

Psalm 33:20

Our soul waits for the LORD; He is our help and our shield.

Almighty Creator God, let the whole world praise You.
Lord, we wait for the day when every knee will bow and
every tongue confess that Jesus is Lord. We wait for You!
God, we desire to see Your Spirit move among us. We
desire to see Your power at work. Only by Your great
power can we fight the powers of Satan and usher people
into Your kingdom. Father, we desire to see You high and
lifted up. We love You Lord. You are our God! We wait for
You! Let Your mercies be upon us Lord. We are desperate
for Your saving grace. We find all our hope in You. Let us
not put any hope in this world Father, but in You alone.
Abba, we love You. Great is Your name. Bless us this day.
Thank You Lord. Alleluia.

Psalm 34:1

I will bless the LORD at all times;
His praise shall continually be in my mouth.

Oh awesome God, You are amazing! Lord, I wish I could
praise You all the day long! You truly are amazing. Let me
never boast in myself or my own accomplishments, but in
Your great work of grace in me. Help me Father to have
Your praise ever be on my lips. I want to praise You at the
store, I want to praise You at my work, and in the car. Lord,
let me not be ashamed of Your gospel! For it is Your gospel
alone that saves! Keep me kingdom minded all day long
Lord! Give me a spirit of worship and let it be contagious so
that all who witness it join with me. God, we want to see
You receive the honor that You deserve. Give me strength
and courage to be that person Lord! Praise Your holy
awesome name! Alleluia!

Psalm 34:4
I sought the LORD, and He heard me,
And delivered me from all my fears

Lord God, You saved me! I was so ridiculously lost and
You came for me. I was on my own path, but You, in Your
goodness, came and brought me home. My heart explodes
with love for You Father. God, You heard me when I called.
You've heard every thought I have ever had. None of my
cries have ever gone unanswered. Lord, thank You for
delivering me from myself! And thank You for saving me
from my foolishness still! God, every day You guide me.
Your Spirit leads me. Holy Spirit, I could not function
without You. Your comfort and Your conviction, Your rod
and Your staff, they comfort me. Lord, Your presence
surrounds me and it comforts me. God, may Your glory be
forever and ever. Praise Your holy name! Bless this day
Father. May all of the glory go to You. Amen.

Psalm 34:9
Oh, fear the LORD, you His saints!
There is no want to those who fear Him.

Father, help me find the divine balances of seeing Your
goodness and Your love for me, while not forgetting that
You are a holy and righteous God. Help me also to fear You
as a wise son fears his father. Lord, You deserve my respect
and adoration. God, Your Word says that to fear You is to
hate evil. Help me to hate evil Father. Holy Spirit, convict
me deeply of my own sins and the sins that surround me in
this world. Give me bold strength to not just sit idly by as
sin abounds around me. Let me not be ashamed of Your
gospel and empower me to denounce the ways of this
world. Lord, as Your servant Dietrich Bonhoeffer said, to be
silent is to not be silent and to not act is to act. Lord help me
to fear You by boldly speaking Your heart. Help me to
honor You. Jesus, be my vision and be my guide. Lead me
in the way everlasting. Amen.

Psalm 35:9
And my soul shall be joyful in the LORD;
It shall rejoice in His salvation.

Oh my soul, rejoice in Your God. Rejoice in His salvation.
Lord, help me to be joyous over Your salvation. Help me to
be joyous over my Savior. Oh God, restore unto me the joy
of Your salvation, and renew a steadfast spirit within me.
Give me that new believer joy again. Give me that new
believer zeal. Let my last days be as zealous as my first.
Light the fire again, within my soul, and let it burn forever
brighter for You Lord. Let Your Word be on my lips and let
my mouth be filled with praise. Lord God, let my life be a
song for You. Let my life be a prayer to You. Let all that I
do show the world my love for You. And Lord, let it all
reflect Your great love for me.

Psalm 35:18
I will give You thanks in the great assembly;
I will praise You among many people.

Lord, I need your help. I desire to be bold before others. I
want to unashamedly declare that You are God and that I
love You. Help me to have courage. Help me to not be
ashamed of the gospel. Lord, take away my pride and my
fears of what other people think. I desire for you to be first
in my life and I want the people around me to absolutely
know that. Help me praise You openly for the many great
blessings You have given me. Let me openly pray to You
and for others without fear of what others make think. Give
me boldness by Your Spirit. Lord Jesus, be Lord of every
part of my life. I pray that my life would bring You glory.
Amen.

Psalm 35:28

And my tongue shall speak of Your righteousness
And of Your praise all the day long.

Father give me boldness to speak of both Your
righteousness and Your praise. Let me not be silent! Lord,
when I don't know what to say, put words in my mouth.
Father, I beg of You to give me the strength to speak. When
I see unrighteousness, when I hear others speak in sin, give
me the strength to rebuke them and speak of Your Holy
Word. Father, let me not be idle. Use me Lord to turn a
generation back to You. And let my time in between be
used to spread Your praise. Let me be quick to speak of
Your mercies. Let me default in conversation to share of
Your amazing blessings. Give me a big heart for You Lord.
Jesus, send Your Spirit to dwell in me in power. Let Your
name be lifted high God. Create in me a clean heart. And
renew my spirit, that I might live boldly for You.
Hallelujah Father.

Psalm 36:7

How precious is Your lovingkindness, O God! Therefore the
children of men put their trust under the shadow of Your wings.

Lord, help me to keep my head on straight! For I know that
Your ways are good, and You would never lead me astray,
yet I do often wander. Lord, I am prone to wander! Prone to
doubt, prone to plot, and prone to do things my way. But
then I remember Your lovingkindness. Oh Lord, Your
lovingkindness is better than life. Therefore God, therefore I
know that it is best to trust You. I come under the shadow
of Your protection. I take heed to Your Word. I trust not in
my own ways, but I look to Your ways. Help Your children
look to You at all times. Help us stay within Your will.
Lord, this world has nothing for us, let us follow You.

Psalm 36:8
They are abundantly satisfied with the fullness of Your house,
And You give them drink from the river of Your pleasures.

Lord, You let us drink from Your river. So often I forget
about just how abundant Your provisions are. Jesus, You
are more than enough for me and You have more than I will
ever need. I never want to question Your provisions. Help
me to trust that You have more than I will ever need and
that You will always give me exactly as much as I need.
Father, You know best. Help me to trust in Your direction,
Your guidance, and Your divine plan for my life. So often I
assume that I know what I need. Help me to just trust in
Your provision and help me to know that You will give me
all that I will ever need. Amen.

Psalm 37:27
Depart from evil, and do good; And dwell forevermore.

Lord God, for Your glory, and Your glory alone, help me to
forsake all evil things. Lord take away any spirit of
compromise I might have. If there is any speck of rebellion
within my heart, I pray that you would take it away. Father I
desire not only to live a holy life for You, but I want to
serve You as well. Give me strength and boldness to
continue to do all the good You have called me to. Help me
to step out and take chances for You. Let me be bold for
you. Lord, I do not want to look back on a life of missed
opportunities. Please send Your Spirit to speak loudly to me
because I often have deaf ears. Burn within me, the desire to
do well in all things. Oh, how I long to hear you say, "well
done" as I enter into Your Kingdom. Keep my eyes on Your
eternal kingdom and do not let me be tempted by the things
of this earth. I love You Jesus. I am grateful for Your
sacrifice and I am humbly speechless before You. Live
inside me Lord and have Your way with me.

Psalm 37:1 & 3

Do not fret because of evildoers, Nor be envious of the workers of iniquity. Trust in the LORD, and do good; Dwell in the land, and feed on His faithfulness.

Father God, You are amazingly faithful to me. When and where I fail, You never fail. You are awesome and worthy of my praise. Father God, help me to not waste any of the precious time that You have given me to be dwelling on the evils that others commit. Help me to spend my time doing good, for Your name's sake, and to be meditating on Your goodness. LORD God, You will bring all things to pass. You will administer justice in Your own time. Father, help me to remember that vengeance belongs to You. I pray God that men would turn to You from their evil ways. Save them Father. Yet if they continue in their ways, let me not dwell on it. There are too many who are hungry for Your Word and Your gospel. Send me to them Father. Use me as Your precious tool today. Let me bring glory to Your name.

Psalm 37:4

Delight yourself also in the LORD, And He shall give you the desires of your heart.

Father God, help me to find my delight in you. Though you bless me with family and friends, though I am provided for in all my needs, help my sole joy come from You. Lord, my friends may fail and my things may break, but you will never fail me. Help me to draw all of my joy from you. Keep my eyes off of the things of this world and keep them focused on You and Your Son. Fill me will Your Holy Spirit and lead me in Your way. Lord, I want You and Your glory to become the desire of my heart. Lord, I know that You will continue to glorify Your name. Empty me of my selfish self and help me to live for you and you alone. Abba, I love You.

Psalm 37:8

Cease from anger, and forsake wrath;
Do not fret--it only causes harm.

Oh God, how prone I am to worry about things. I often lose
track of how small my problems are in comparison to how
great and awesome You are. Help me not to fret. Lord do
not let my anxieties build within me. Help me to hand them
over to You. Lord, my anxieties do often lure me to a spirit
of anger, and my anger to wrath. God, I do not desire to
have any part in unrighteous wrath. Give me a spirit of
peace. Give me patience to deal with those around me. Help
me to be a beacon of hope for those who see me. Father I
desire to point people to You in everything that I do. Help
me, and give me the strength, to trust in You for all things
great and small. Let me feel Your love Father. Amen.

Psalm 37:23-24

The steps of a good man are ordered by the LORD, And He
delights in his way. Though he fall, he shall not be utterly
cast down; For the LORD upholds him with His hand

Father, You hold my tears in a bottle, You order my steps
before me, and You hold me in Your hand. God, I do
stumble and fall. And I often find myself broken. Yet You
have ordered my steps? You knew I would stumble. You
knew I would fall. You knew it all before it would happen,
but You also know that I do delight in You. My foolish
heart may wander, but it always finds its way home. Oh
Lord, I love You. I am so very comforted knowing that
though I may stumble, You never cast me out. For me and
all that come to You, You by no means cast out. You
uphold us with Your mighty hand. You protect us with
Your outstretched arm. You are so very good to us Lord.
You do not forsake Your people. Praise the name of Jesus.
All glory and praise be Yours. Amen.

Psalm 37:39-40

But the salvation of the righteous is from the LORD; He is their strength in the time of trouble. And the LORD shall help them and deliver them; He shall deliver them from the wicked, And save them, Because they trust in Him.

God, You truly have given me a simple task, yet it can be so hard at times. Oh that I would learn to trust You more. To trust You in all things. To commend all my ways to Your great wisdom. Lord, You have promised to be my strength in times of trouble. You have promised to deliver me from the evil one. You have promised to save me. Oh the riches that are in Christ! How greatly You bless us! And now let me trust in You. Lord, deliver me from my self! My self, my flesh, my own craftiness, and all of my independent ways. Lord, let me live a life dependent on You. Help me to trust You Lord. Enable me to lay down my own strength and trust in Your help alone. Your ways are so much better Lord. Here I am God. Take me and make me Yours.

Psalm 38:3-5

There is no soundness in my flesh Because of Your anger, Nor any health in my bones Because of my sin. For my iniquities have gone over my head; Like a heavy burden they are too heavy for me. My wounds are foul and festering Because of my foolishness.

"O wretched man that I am!" Lord, I pray with Paul. Who will save me from this body of sin and death? Father, I am to please You, yet I often stumble and fall. I have come to realize that there is no good thing in me. I have nothing to offer You except this empty vessel. And yet while I am so broken, I feel as if I am coming to where You want me to be. Totally emptied of myself and utterly reliant on You. There is nothing left for me to give You. You are my God and I cry out to You, "save me!" I love You Lord. I know that You know how much my heart longs for You, yet my flesh battles against me. Help me to walk in Your Spirit Lord. I need to be full of You and emptied of myself. Not my will be done Lord, but Yours alone. Amen.

Psalm 38:9
Lord, all my desire is before You;
And my sighing is not hidden from You.

Jesus, help me to seek You in all things. Do not let me
needlessly worry about the things in my life which You
desire to bear for me. I want to lay all my struggles at Your
feet and I want my heart to seek after You first. I want to
seek You in the morning and rest with You in the evening.
Be my God from wake until sleep. God, You see all things
and You know the things I struggle and dwell over. Show
me how to give them over to You and how to trust in Your
guidance. Let me find peace and rest in You.
Oh Yahweh, You are my God.

Psalm 38:21-22
Do not forsake me, O LORD; O my God, be not far from
me! Make haste to help me, O Lord, my salvation!

God, I need You here with me. I need to feel Your presence.
I need to feel the moving of Your Spirit once more. Where
did I go? Why did I wander? I cannot even remember what
happened? Yet now I know, I need You more than ever. You
taught me a lesson Lord. Life is miserable without You. The
things my flesh longs for leave me empty. My laziness only
leads to regret. Oh God, be near to me now! Reveal Yourself
to me in Your Word! Remind me of Your wonderful
promises. Your Word, Lord, I have hidden it in my heart!
Let it shine forth now and bring me comfort. Remind this
sinner of Your ways and remind me of Your promises. Lord
God, remind me of this blessed truth, "There is therefore
now no condemnation to those who are in Christ Jesus." Let
me walk in Your ways Lord. Let me walk in Your Spirit.
Keep me by Your side and hold me in Your arms. I love
You Lord, and I lift my voice to worship You. Amen.

Psalm 39:4

LORD, make me to know my end, And what is the measure
of my days, That I may know how frail I am.

Father God, help me redeem the time. I live in an age of
endless distractions. I can so easily become focused on
things that truly have little value. My generation seeks after
entertainment, while the world around us is soon going to
burn. Lord, help me count my days. I do not want to waste
this life that You have redeemed. I have wasted too long
chasing after sin and the cares of this world, let me redeem
what time is left to the souls for Your kingdom and to bring
honor to Your Name. Keep my eyes fixed upon the cross of
Jesus Christ and do not let me walk in fear. Let me walk in
love, for there is no fear in love. Help me live for You Lord.
Guide Your servant and show me what You would have me
do. Praise You Father. Hallelujah.

Psalm 39:7

And now, Lord, what do I wait for? My hope is in You.

God, sometimes I feel like I just don't get it. What am I
waiting for? Why do I give You any less than my all? Lord,
You are my hope and my shield! Help me to run this race of
life with integrity and zeal. You deserve my whole life.
Help me to give it to you freely and cheerfully. Lord, give
me the confidence I need. Remind me of Your goodness.
Remind me of Your great promises. Do not let me be fooled
by what this world has to offer me. Burn like a fire in my
heart. Let me live for Your glory and Your fame. Let me
proudly boast in the victory that I have received through
Christ. Jesus, You are the way, the truth, and the light!
Draw me close to You. Amen.

Psalm 39:12

Hear my prayer, O LORD, And give ear to my cry; Do not be silent at my tears; For I am a stranger with You, A sojourner, as all my fathers were.

Oh Lord, You hear my prayers! You hear me Lord! You see the broken spirit and You hear the longing heart. You know when we pray empty words of religious nonsense, but You also hear the groanings of a speechless heart. Lord God, we come to You. I come to You Lord. Hear my prayers this day. Hear all that I cry out to You. I cannot even put into words the things that I need God, but You know them nonetheless. You know my every need. You know my every pain. Lord God, You have counted all my tears and You hold them in Your bottle. Nothing goes unnoticed by You Lord. I am never forsaken. I am never destitute when I call out to You. Father, please help me. You know what I need even better than I do. You know the true needs of this desperate soul. Let me entrust this day to You. You rule and reign in my life this day and I will trust that Your will will be done in my life. Give me ears that hear. Give me hands that serve. Give me feet that follow. Help me to live for You today.

Psalm 40:5

Many, O LORD my God, are Your wonderful works Which You have done; And Your thoughts toward us Cannot be recounted to You in order; If I would declare and speak of them, They are more than can be numbered.

Lord, my memory is often so weak. You have saved me time and time again. You have provided for me more than I could have ever deserved. One day I will see all of the pain You have protected me from without my knowing. Yet, I continually forget. Sometimes the smallest mishap can lead me to question Your goodness. Far be it from me Lord! Revive my mind! Help me to remember the great works You have done in me! Help me remember the mountains we once stood on and get me through these valleys! Father, forgive me of my forgetfulness and lack of faith at times. Forgive my backslidings. Help me remember all that You have done for me. Jesus, keep my eyes on You and Your cross that You bore for me. Let me not forget that my sins are nailed upon it. Replace my spirit of self-condemnation with a spirit of joy for all that You have done! Great are Your works Father! Great is Your love for me Jesus! Holy Spirit, let me never forget that You are in me. Let me feel Your presence. Let me listen to Your guidance.

Psalm 40:17

But I am poor and needy; Yet the LORD thinks upon me.
You are my help and my deliverer; Do not delay, O my God.

Who am I, Oh God? Who am I, that the Creator God of the
heavens and the earth would love me? Who am I, that the
Sinless One would send His Son to die on my behalf? Who
am I, that the One whose voice broke up the fountain of the
deep would speak to me? Who am I, that He who knows all
things, from beginning to end, would choose to think of
me? Lord God, who am I, that though I sin and fall, again
and again, and though I wander far from Your will, You
still call me Your friend? Oh Lord my God, I know who I
am. I am poor and needy; yet You, Oh God, still think of
me. Praise Your holy name Father. Be magnified above all
else. Lord, You are my King, and I live to follow You.
Blessed be Your name.

Psalm 41:1

Blessed is he who considers the poor;
The LORD will deliver him in time of trouble.

Father, from cover to cover in Your Word You exhort us to
care for the poor, for the orphan and the widow. I pray that
Your Church continues to meet the needs of the less
fortunate. I pray that I never become jaded or impartial to
those who need Your love. This world has become full of
swindlers and idle people. It makes it so easy for me to want
to cease all efforts to give aid because I think it will be in
vain. Yet I need to remain open to the voice of Your Spirit.
Help me to be discerning with those who seek need. Help
me to neither enable the dishonest, nor withhold aid from
those who are truly in need. And above all else Lord, help
me to share with them the greatest gift that meets their
greatest need, the message of the cross and of Your Son.

Psalm 41:4
I said, "LORD, be merciful to me;
Heal my soul, for I have sinned against You."

Lord God, day by day I seek to please You. I long to be
acceptable before Your eyes Father. Yet in this body of
sinful flesh, no good thing dwells. My flesh wars against
my spirit and I often stumble in my walk with You. Father,
continue to show Your great mercy towards me. Wash me
daily in Your Word and by the blood of Your Son. Remind
me Lord, that I am continually being made new, by Your
great mercies alone. Let me not fall into condemnation by
the lies of the evil one. Let me not beat myself up for those
things which Your Son was beaten for. For He truly was
bruised for my transgressions. Lord God, again I say,
cleanse me from my sin and keep me forever before Your
face. Guide me day by day and help me to be a blessing to
You. I pray that my life would bring You, my everlasting
Father, great joy. I love You Lord. Keep me close by Your
side.

Psalm 42:1-2
As the deer pants for the water brooks, So pants my soul for
You, O God. My soul thirsts for God, for the living God.
When shall I come and appear before God?

Lord, this world often distracts me from You. I often find
myself so busy. But when the things around me settle, I am
reminded of my longing for You. Oh, to just feel Your
presence warms my soul. I truly do thirst for You Jesus.
This world is dry and You bring me great refreshment. I
long for the day when I will stand before You and all other
things will pass away. I do not desire to ever lose sight of
You, but this world throws so many things at me. Help me
to keep my peace and to be Your ambassador. Help me
hallow Your name in all that I do. Thank You Father.

Psalm 42:5

Why are you cast down, O my soul? And why are you disquieted within me? Hope in God, for I shall yet praise Him For the help of His countenance.

Father, why do I ever feel troubled? How does anxiety ever take hold of me? Why do my eyes ever wander from You? It is only then that I fear, when my eyes are off You. As long as I keep my hope in You, I have no fear. When my trust is in You, my joy is full. Teach me Lord, to ever hope in You. Fill me with Your truth and Your love. Keep my eyes ever fixed upon You and lead me in the way everlasting. Lord, I pray that my countenance would be a testimony of Your work in my life. When hard times come, I want to hold fast so that others can see that those who hope in the Lord will not fall. Those who hope in the Lord will be lifted up, encouraged, and strengthened. Let me be the one who points people to You through the testimony of my blessed hope.

Psalm 43:3

Oh, send out Your light and Your truth! Let them lead me; Let them bring me to Your holy hill And to Your tabernacle.

Oh Lord, send me Your light and truth! Let them surround me. I want to feel Your power in my life. Keep me in Your Word, let it dwell within my heart and have it guide my steps. Give me a hunger for Your Word and a thirst for Your righteousness. Holy Spirit illuminate the wicked world around me. People continue to call evil good and good evil. Let Your light shine in this earth during dark times. Father, by Your Word and the illumination of Your Spirit, bring me into close fellowship with You. I want to draw near to You and feel Your arms surround me. Comfort me Lord. Give me Your peace. Thank You for Your sacrifice. You are so, so good. Amen.

Psalm 43:5

Why are you cast down, O my soul? And why are you disquieted within me? Hope in God; For I shall yet praise Him, The help of my countenance and my God.

Oh my soul, how fickle you can be! Lord, why did You make us so? One day I feel as if I could sprint up Your holy mountain and it seems as if only moments later I find myself in the pit. I walk in Your Spirit Lord, yet it is as if I walk on a knife's edge. One moment I am in bliss and then suddenly I lose sight of You. When I get my eyes off of You and on to me I quickly fall. Oh Lord, let me never lose sight of You. Keep my hope in You and You alone. Do not let me deceive myself to think that I could ever be good enough. I rest in Your mercy and grace alone. My hope is in God, not in me! And God, You cannot fail! What have I to fear? Lord, it is when my eyes are on me that I despair. Let my eyes never wander from Your throne. You alone guide me. You alone can save me. Lord God, You alone are worthy of my praise. Blessed be Your holy name Father. Hallelujah.

Psalm 44:1

We have heard with our ears, O God, Our fathers have told us, The deeds You did in their days, In days of old

Oh Mighty God, I have read the stories in Your Word. I have been told of the great works You have done in generations past. I read them Lord, but my eyes have not seen them. Lord God, throughout history You have moved in seasons. There have been seasons of little and seasons of plenty. Father, I beg of You, I have heard of the revivals that You brought our fathers, Lord God, do it again! One last time father, move as You have countless times before. Show Yourself strong on behalf of Your people. Send Your Holy Spirit to move within Your Church. Let there be one last gathering of all peoples unto You. Lord, we need it. We cannot go on without it. Send revival to Your church. Let us not be a generation that has never seen a mighty moving of the Spirit of God. In these final hours of Your great plan, cleanse Your bride, empower her, and use her to draw in a great harvest of souls. Lord, we need Your reviving power within us. Come and save us.

Psalm 44:6-8

For I will not trust in my bow, Nor shall my sword save me. But You have saved us from our enemies, And have put to shame those who hated us. In God we boast all day long, And praise Your name forever.

Lord help me to surrender ALL to You. I do not even realize all of the ways that I try to take my fate and my life into my own hands. Help me to trust in You and to let You control the steps of my life. Father let my job, my income, my health, my choices, my family, and all things be laid at Your feet. Let me hand them over to You for You to control. Help me to never become proud over my accomplishments, as if You were not sustaining me at all times. Help me to boast in You and Your great works. Help me boast in the great provisions of my great God! Let me be known as a worshipper. Let me be known for my great and zealous love of You. Let my life bring You praise and glory! You are amazing and You are so long-suffering towards me. Thank You for Your amazing, unending, and abounding grace.

Psalm 45:1

My heart is overflowing with a good theme; I recite my composition concerning the King; My tongue is the pen of a ready writer.

Oh great and mighty God, let Your praise ever be on my lips. Let Your song ever be on my tongue. Lord, let my hands always be busy with the tasks that You have set them to. Let my feet walk firmly upon the path that You have guided them on. Lord, let my eyes forever be fixed upon Your throne and the heavens. Eternally focused on the things that have eternal value. Let my knees be bent often in humble prayer to You. Let my shoulders feel unburdened, knowing that Your yoke is easy, and it is by grace that I am saved. Lord, let Your Spirit dwell within me. May my body be Its temple. Father God, let my heart be broken for what breaks Your heart, yet full of Your everlasting joy. Lord God, let my whole life be a song that is pleasant to Your ears. Take pleasure in Your servant. Receive joy from Your child. I live for You and You alone. Bless You Father, bless You.

Psalm 45:17

I will make Your name to be remembered in all generations;
Therefore the people shall praise You forever and ever.

King Jesus! Oh, how I long for the day when Your name is forever on my lips. Let alone the lips of every man, woman, and child. Lord, You are amazing. Help me to remember Your great name. Help me to call upon the power found in Your name. Truly let Your name be on my lips when I rise and when I lay to sleep. God, Your name is great and powerful and often I forget it. Draw my heart to You Jesus. Bring me close into Your presence. Let me speak Your name with boldness to all who will hear. Let me bring glory to Your great name. Jesus, hallowed be Your name! King Jesus, let Your will be done in my life and on this earth! Christ Jesus, provide for me and keep me close so that others can see the power of Your name. Lord Jesus, keep me from my temptations, deliver me from my flesh, so that Your name would not be blasphemed. Oh, my Jesus. All glory to You. All power is Yours. You are my King. Hallelujah.

Psalm 46:1-2

God is our refuge and strength, A very present help in
trouble. Therefore we will not fear, Even though the earth
be removed, And though the mountains be carried into the
midst of the sea

God, you are powerful and mighty. You are great and you are strong. Let my eyes ever be fixed upon you, so that even if the world is crashing down around me, I see the pillar of Your great strength providing my shelter. Lord, the enemy desires to throw all he can at me, but I need to keep my focus on You. With You by my side, leading me on, I can face anything! Jesus, through Your power in me, I can face all things. Oh Lord, let me never forget this. I forget Your promises daily because I am merely man, but You bring me back to them. Let me dwell in Your Word so that I never lose my focus. Help me to remember, hour by hour, that the Maker of the heavens and the earth loves me and is protecting me. Thank you for Your great love.

Psalm 46:10

*Be still, and know that I am God; I will be exalted among
the nations, I will be exalted in the earth!*

Father, I run to and fro, day in and day out. Remind me to
be still and focus on You Lord. Do not let a day go by
where I have not meditated on Your amazing grace, Your
unending mercy, and Your great sacrifice You gave for me.
Jesus, help me look to the day when every knee will bow
and every tongue will confess You as Lord over all the
earth. I long for the day when all will exalt You. Until that
day comes, let me bring glory to Your name in all that I do.
Let my hands be Yours, let my feet be Yours, and let my
heart forever be Yours Lord. Guide my steps today and lead
me down the paths that You desire. Let me be ever obedient
to Your calling on my life. Help me to be still and
remember that You are God.

Psalm 47:1

*Oh, clap your hands, all you peoples!
Shout to God with the voice of triumph!*

Oh great King, You do rule and reign over this earth. Your
creation is in Your hands and all things are under Your
control. I thank You Lord that in all of Your glory You still
think of me. I humbly come before You Father to sing Your
praise. You are awesome and mighty! Your glories know no
end. Your mercies are from everlasting to everlasting.
Praise You Lord for all of Your awesome goodness. No
matter what troubles may face me, or trials may come, I
know that You are still in control. You are awesome and
most blessed God. You are unchanging and undefeatable!
You are powerful and omnipotent! You are the King of all
kings and the Lord of all lords. You are my God!

Psalm 47:6-7

Sing praises to God, sing praises! Sing praises to our King, sing praises! For God is the King of all the earth; Sing praises with understanding.

Lord, let me always sing praises to You. You are worthy to be praised and while I often focus on the problems that surround me, I must keep my eyes focused on You because You are forever on the throne. Help me to embrace in my inner self the fact that You still reign over this earth. All things are in Your hands and so I should rejoice. Help me to go through my day praising You. Help me to sing praises to my King in the presence of all who will hear. Let me point them to You and Your great mercy and love. Praise You Jesus! You alone are King, forever and ever. Amen!

Psalm 48:9

We have thought, O God, on Your lovingkindness, In the midst of Your temple.

Your love towards me, Oh God, is never-ending. If I were to write of Your love, the books would surpass the mountains. If I were to store Your love for me, it would overflow the storehouses of heaven. Oceans cannot contain the great flood of love that You pour out on Your children. How many are your loving thoughts towards me, oh Lord? They outnumber the sands of the sea. Even the stars of the sky cannot match Your wonderful thoughts towards me! Who am I, that the Almighty God, Creator of heaven and earth, should love me so? I am less than nothing before You Lord, yet I hold an amazing value, because I am Yours. Without You I would be like smoke in the wind, yet through Your grace You have made me an heir. You love is so very good Father. Thank You for ever loving me so.

Psalm 48:14
For this is God, Our God forever and ever;
He will be our guide Even To death.

Lord, I will follow You, even unto death. You point the way and I will march onward. Lord, be the wind in my sails. I want to run for You, I want to build for You, and I want to live for You. From this day forth and on into eternity, You are the Lord of my life. Let me not be ashamed of the gospel of Your Son Jesus. Let me put all of my trust into Your guidance. Wherever You take me, I know that You are working all things together for Your glory and for my good. God, I want to live with abandon and without a shred of doubt. I want to soar on the wings of eagles and boldly go forth declaring Your great and holy name. You are amazing Father! Let the whole world hear! Let us sing the praises of Your Son Jesus. Let every man, woman, and child know of His great name and let every knee bow before Him. Jesus, You are my King! Let me bring glory, honor, and praise to Your Name this day. Fill me with the power of Your Holy Spirit and let the whole world declare that Christ is Lord! HALLELUJAH!

Psalm 49:2
Both low and high, Rich and poor together.

Lord God, in all of my ways and in all of my days, let me live for You. God, when you uplift me to the tops of mountains, let me sing Your praise. And when You take me down to the lowest valleys, let me understand Your vision for me. When I have all of my needs abundantly met, let me praise You for Your goodness. When I am needy and poor, let me trust in Your provision. Whether high or low, hot or cold, rich or poor, let me always reverence You with a pure heart. Even in my darkest trials, let me cry out to You alone. Your hand is upon me Lord. You know what it is that I need and what I desire. You have formed me for a task in Your kingdom, let that be the goal of my life. No matter where You take me, no matter what occurs, help me to forever look to You, my God and my King. All glory be Yours God, forever and ever, amen.

Psalm 49:6-7

Those who trust in their wealth And boast in the multitude of their riches, None of them can by any means redeem his brother, Nor give to God a ransom for him

Lord God, You and You alone have saved me. Let me give You my life as a living sacrifice. I desire to live for you and you alone. Father, the world around me is perishing. They seek riches, pleasure, and fame and Your gospel is foolishness to them. Please open their eyes! Help them to come to Your truth. Remove the veil that the enemy has placed over their hearts. Help them to come to know their loving Father and their Savior. They go through the days seeking all things except You. Help them to see that true joy comes through You alone. Let me not be silent Lord. Help me be obedient to Your Word and give me the strength I need to be Your witness in this world.

Psalm 50:5

Gather My saints together to Me, Those who have made a covenant with Me by sacrifice.

Lord, I wait for the day when You will call me home. This world seems to be falling apart, but You have taught us that it is truly falling into place. You will come for us. You will not let things go too far before You gather us to You. Until that time God, please lead me and guide me. Help me to number my days and consciously place my steps. I want to be used by You with what little time I have left to give. Whether for a day or a year, I want my days to be lived out for Your glory. Help me never to forget how precious each day You give me is. My life is not my own! For You have purchased me by the sacrifice of Your Son. Help me to live as one of the redeemed. Help me to live as one who has received costly grace. Help me God, to live for You.

Psalm 50:15

Call upon Me in the day of trouble; I will deliver you, and you shall glorify Me.

Oh God, I fall into trouble and temptation often, yet I am slow to look to You for help. Remind me Lord, to call on Your great name in my weakness. Do not let me stumble in my moments of trouble. Hold me in Your arms. Let Your love and Your power surround me. Restrain me from my foolish ways. Father, please keep me from sinning against You. Give me the power to live a holy life for you that brings honor and glory to Your name. Let my life hallow Your great name. I only desire to bring You honor and glory. But Lord, if I do stumble, if I fall and give into my sin, help me to look to Your Son. Jesus, You have paid the price. Do not let my failures be followed by the lie of condemnation. For You are my Redeemer! Though I may fall back into the mud, You continually make me white as snow. Do not let my failures hold me down. Let me place them at the foot of the cross, where You bore them all Lord Jesus. God, I give You my life. Be with me this day. This new day that You have given me. And let me live for You. Amen Lord.

Psalm 51:1

Have mercy upon me, O God, According to Your lovingkindness; According to the multitude of Your tender mercies, Blot out my transgressions.

Oh Lord, forgive me of all my failures, wash away my sin, and remind me that by Your blood I am made as white as snow. I know that I am far from perfect, except how I am found in Your Son. Aside of through You Jesus, I am nothing. God, it is You alone Whom I fail. But Lord, let me never forget Your mercies, let me never forget Your great love, and never let me forget the great price You paid so that I could stand before You faultless. Help me live my life as one of the redeemed. Let me bring glory and honor to Your name and give me the strength to remember that I am forgiven.

Psalm 51:2

Wash me thoroughly from my iniquity, And cleanse me from my sin.

Oh LORD God, please forgive me, a sinner. Lord, I have sinned against You and I have broken Your law. Forgive me Father. My heart is so rebellious, yet it breaks over my sin. I am broken before You. Lord, I trust in Your great salvation, through Your Son Jesus, but I condemn myself. Do not let me fall into condemnation, nor let me continue to walk in sin. Help restore Your child and renew my heart. Cleanse me Father and purge out all of my wickedness. My deepest desire is to live wholly for You. Take me Lord, use me, and watch over me. Keep me from sin. Amen.

Psalm 51:6

Behold, You desire truth in the inward parts,
And in the hidden part You will make me to know wisdom.

O God, You see my depths and my darkness. Those things
which are hidden inside of me, You see as if they were
standing in the noonday sun. Nothing is hidden from You.
Lord, You see the sins inside of me more clearly than I see
them myself. LORD God, I beg of You, show me the sins
which even I do not see. Reveal to me my own wickedness
and then give me the power to repent of them all. I want to
be a pure vessel for You Lord. I want to be holy as You are
holy. When the enemy tries to condemn me of my sin, I will
only claim the righteousness that is found in Jesus Christ.
You are my righteousness Lord. You alone! Lord God,
search me, reveal to me, cleanse me, and empower me to
walk in Your Spirit day by day. Thank You Lord.

Psalm 51:8

Make me hear joy and gladness,
That the bones You have broken may rejoice.

"Make me hear joy and gladness, That the bones You have
broken may rejoice." Yes Lord! Let me have Your joy!
Bring to me Your gladness! Let my heart overflow with
Your praises. Lord, show me Your ways. I know now that
what You have done is good. Lord, these bones which You
have allowed to be broken were for my good. You chastise
me because You love me. While my pain is temporary,
Your gifts are eternal. My pain is for but a moment, but
Lord, Your Son was broken for my iniquity. I am clean! I
am new! I am reborn! Like life itself, all of these trials are
but a vapor in comparison to Your great blessings. Lord,
You are so good to me. Help me to never forget that You
are working in me, to will and to do Your good pleasure. It
is You Lord who are completing the good work which You
started in me. Take me Lord! Take my life and break these
bones if need be. I am Yours for the molding.

Psalm 51:10

Create in me a clean heart, O God,
And renew a steadfast spirit within me.

Lord, I know You will never leave me, You will never
forsake me, and You will never cast me off, but Lord, keep
me near You so I do not sin against You. I want to feel
Your Holy Spirit in me and working through me. Lord, do
not take away Your Spirit from me, do not remove my
candlestick, I desire to be a light for You. Jesus, I want my
joy for You today to burn as fervent as it ever has. Even
brighter Lord, I desire to burn hot for You. Father, when I
am weak and unable to carry on, please uphold me by Your
generous Spirit. Father, send us Your Promise so that we
can teach the lost Your ways, so that we can be witnesses of
Your Son and His death, burial, and resurrection. We desire
to see sinners turn to You Father. Help us, enable us, and
empower us.

Psalm 51:11-12

Do not cast me away from Your presence, And do not take
Your Holy Spirit from me. Restore to me the joy of Your
salvation, And uphold me by Your generous Spirit.

Lord, keep me away from anything that would keep me
from You. Take me back to where I have fallen from, back
to the glory of Your presence. Let my heart yearn for You
again. Let me long to be in Your presence. In the night
hours I will seek You. While the world is still, I will hear
Your voice again. Create a clean heart within me, O God,
and take not Your Holy Spirit from me. Cast me not away
from Your presence. And renew me Lord, to the person I
once was, the person I long to be, one after God's own heart.
I love You Lord and I always will. Keep me forever by
Your side. Amen.

Psalm 51:13

Then I will teach transgressors Your ways,
And sinners shall be converted to You.

Father God, open my mouth and let me pour out praises to You. Unbind my tongue and let me teach sinners Your ways. Remove my fear from me and help me to shout forth Your wonderful works. God, use me to lead others to Christ. That they might see the glory and magnificence of Your Son. Use me God! You formed me in my mother's womb and You made me with a purpose. My life has a calling on it and I want to be used for that purpose. Help me to build Your kingdom. Help me to see Your name be hallowed on the earth. Give me words to speak so that others will come to know You. God You are loving and kind.

You are so gracious and merciful. You are longsuffering towards us. Help me to show the world who You are. Loose my lips Lord. Make me Your herald. Remove my fear and pour out Your Spirit upon me. Thank You for hearing my prayers Abba. To You be all glory and honor and praise.

Psalm 51:16-17

For You do not desire sacrifice, or else I would give it; You do not delight in burnt offering. The sacrifices of God are a broken spirit, A broken and a contrite heart - These, O God, You will not despise.

Lord God, here I am, all of me. Take me, use me, and put an obedient heart within me that lives to serve You alone. Father, mold me into whatever You see fit and use me as You sovereignly desire. Lord, I can make nothing for You, in and of myself. All I have to offer is the life that You have given me, so Lord, take my life and let it be wholly Yours. Give me a heart that weeps over my sin and the lost. Give me a heart full of love for both believers and the lost. Whatever You desire of me, have Your way. I am utterly and completely Yours. Thank You for Your great peace, thank You for Your Son, and thank you for the power You give me through Your Spirit. You are good Lord, You are good.

75

Psalm 52:1

Why do you boast in evil, O mighty man?
The goodness of God endures continually.

Father God, open the eyes of the blind. No, not the blind
physically, but the spiritually blind whom I see throughout
my day. It creates a stirring inside of me when I see them
rejoice in lewdness and iniquity. Lord, they laugh at what
You loathe. Father God, let them see a glimpse of Your
goodness. Help them to see the error of their ways. There is
nothing but death down that path. They keep on trying to fill
the void in their hearts, but only You bring the peace that
surpasses understanding. God, let me be a model of this
peace. Let my life be a testimony of the goodness of the
Lord. God, Your mercies are forever and ever. Thank You
for saving me. Amen.

Psalm 52:8-9

But I am like a green olive tree in the house of God; I trust
in the mercy of God forever and ever. I will praise You
forever, Because You have done it; And in the presence of
Your saints I will wait on Your name, for it is good.

Jesus, You have done it! My victory is won! I have no fears
because You have already won the battle. Let me live as one
who has already won the prize. Do not let me wallow
through this life as though I have pain and sorrows. God,
You have given me life and life abundant! Let me sing
praises to You in the streets, in the stores, and on the
highway. God, I want all to know that I am a child of the
One True King! I love You Lord. You have planted me,
water me, and You continue to grow me. Let Your praises
never cease from my lips. Let all know that You are my
King, You are my Provider, You are my Strength, and You
are my Savior! Jesus, I adore You! Father, I love You! Holy
Spirit, every moment of every hour, I need You! Hallelujah,
praise be to my great God!

Psalm 53:2

God looks down from heaven upon the children of men, To see if there are any who understand, who seek God.

Lord Jesus, I long for Your return. These last days are full of unbelief and wickedness. The hearts of men grow cold, they deny Your name, and they deny even Your existence. They are fools Lord! And they love their foolish ways. We are mocked for walking in Your ways and every day it seems like another good thing is being called evil and evil thing called good. Help me to stand fast and finish strong. Give me the strength to be different and to stand up for Your Word and Your Son. Lord give me boldness to be a witness of Your cross. I need Your Spirit upon me every single day. Without Your power in me I cannot accomplish anything. Maranatha, dear Lord, please come quickly! Bless You Lord!

Psalm 54:1

Save me, O God, by Your name, And vindicate me by Your strength.

Oh Lord my God, by Your name I have found peace. I have everlasting peace through salvation and Your great supernatural peace to keep me until You call me home. Lord God, it is by Your name alone that I am saved. It is only by the name of Jesus that I can pray this prayer. Through Jesus I have all I need in this life. Lord God, it is by Your strength alone that I am saved. Too often I will try to do things through my own strength, but I become exhausted every time. Thank You Lord for saving me by Your great strength. Lord, I rest in Your loving arms. Again Lord, thank You for everything. I am forever grateful for Your amazing loving kindness.

Psalm 54:6
I will freely sacrifice to You; I will praise Your name,
O LORD, for it is good.

God, give me a heart of thanks. Let me praise You all day
long. I want to be a testimony to the great peace and joy
You give Your children. You have not given me a spirit of
fear, or doubt, or anger, but of love, joy, peace,
longsuffering, kindness, goodness, faithfulness, and self-
control. Let these things be in me! I want my entire life to
be a sacrifice for You! I want all of my works to be like a
sweet incense that brings You joy. Father, help me to give
my life and my possessions without fear or remorse. Lord
Jesus, help me to look to You for all that I do. You are my
great Model. You are my fearless Captain.
You are my King!

Psalm 55:12-15
For it is not an enemy who reproaches me; Then I could bear
it. Nor is it one who hates me who has exalted himself against
me; Then I could hide from him. But it was you, a man my
equal, My companion and my acquaintance. We took sweet
counsel together, And walked to the house of God in the
throng. Let death seize them; Let them go down alive into hell,
For wickedness is in their dwellings and among them.

Lord Jesus, teach me how to forgive. Put Your heart inside
of me because that is the only way I can bear the pain of
betrayal. To be mocked and scorned by the wicked I can
understand, but to be hurt by my friends or family is so
hard. That those whom I care about most would try to do
me harm. Father, forgive them, and teach me how to forgive
them too. Lord, I know that they must be hurting because
people do not act in cruel ways when they are filled with
joy. Fill them with Your joy Lord! Fill them with Your
love! Give me the strength to be like You Jesus and to turn
the other cheek. Let me repay their evil with Your great
love. Fill me Spirit. Help me. Amen.

Psalm 55:16-17

As for me, I will call upon God, And the LORD shall save me. Evening and morning and at noon I will pray, and cry aloud, And He shall hear my voice.

God, I wish I sought You as often as I know that I should. I should seek You every morning, look to You for a refill every noon, and rest with You as I lay each night. Help me to continually be lifting prayers to You. Help me to seek You for every need and for every decision. Lord, I know that You hear me when I call. You hear my cries and You know my every thought. And Lord, I know in my head that You hear me, but help me to know it in my heart. Let me believe to my core that the Lord of the universe, Creator God, hears my every call, and desires a relationship with me. Father, let me morning, noon, and night bring You my prayers, my praises, and all my needs. Let me trust that You hear me. And let Your peace, that goes beyond all understanding, guard my heart and mind. Thank You Father.

Psalm 56:3-4

Whenever I am afraid, I will trust in You. In God (I will praise His word), In God I have put my trust; I will not fear. What can flesh do to me?

God, if you are for me, who can be against me?!?! Let that sink into my bones. That God Almighty is on my side! Help me filter each day and each passing moment through the promises of Your Word. You Word brings me hope. Your Word brings me peace. When I feel weak, the promises of Your Word show me how to be strong. Oh Lord, above all else, let me never forget that You hear me when I call. That I have never once been left alone. That you have kept track of every tear and every cry. Hear me oh Lord! I cry out to You once again. Fill me afresh with Your Spirit and lead me this day down the path You have set before me. Thank You Abba Father for always being there for me. Help me to be there for You. Amen.

Psalm 56:10-11

In God (I will praise His Word), In the LORD (I will praise His Word), In God I have put my trust; I will not be afraid. What can man do to me?

God, You have set numerous blessings before me in Your Word. Your promises are bountiful and Your Word beautiful. I have all these things in which I can find my peace. God, I praise You for Your Word, my sure foundation, and Your promises, my everlasting hope. Satan would have me fear man, but You, O God, tell me to not be afraid of what man can do. Father God, help me to trust in Your promises. Help me to lean not on my own understanding. Ground me in Your Word and hide it in my heart, that I might not fear man and sin against You. Lord, if You are for me, and Your promises true, what can man do to me? No, I will fear no man and I will fear no evil. You are with me God. You demonstrate Your love for me and remind me of it every day. You are my strong tower, my rock, and my shield. You are my everything. Praise You Father. Hallelujah.

Psalm 57:1

Be merciful to me, O God, be merciful to me! For my soul trusts in You; And in the shadow of Your wings I will make my refuge, Until these calamities have passed by.

Lord, never let the trials of this earth overshadow Your awesome power. Lord Jesus, the only way I can bear this life is if I cling closer to You than I do my problems. Though my troubles may seem great, my God is greater! Lord, You will once again save me, as You always have! Lord, send down Your grace, Your mercy, and Your truth. Give me the peace that surpasses understanding and guard my heart and my mind. Lord, let me be an ambassador of Your great peace. Let those around me come to know Your great peace through me. Help me to show the world that our God saves! Be high and lifted up Lord Jesus! And by Your Spirit, help me to bring honor and glory to Your name. Hallelujah!

Psalm 57:7

My heart is steadfast, O God, my heart is steadfast;
I will sing and give praise.

Oh Lord, my heart is fixed on You! Though my energy
wanes and my fervor frequently fades, Lord, You have my
heart. Sin seduces me and the world wearies me, but my
heart belongs to You. Father, help me to crucify my flesh
which fights against my heart's desire! I long to love You. I
long to live for You. I'd give you my every breath if I could.
Lord, I know and You know how fickle I can be, but You
also know my one desire, to know You more. Oh Lord, my
sin separates, but You restore. My flesh fights against me,
but You carry me onward. Lord God, let my heart be
forever fixed upon You. Fixed upon Your Word, Your
Ways, Your Spirit, and You blessed Son Jesus. Oh God,
take my heart and let it be, consecrated Lord to Thee.

Psalm 58:11

So that men will say, "Surely there is a reward for the
righteous; Surely He is God who judges in the earth."

Lord, help me to remain heavenly minded. Being a mere
human, I fix my eyes on this life, but I desire to have a heart
and mind that are focused on the life to come. Lord, Your
Word says that nothing done in Your name will be in vain.
Thank You for Your promises. Help me to rest each night,
knowing that You know my labors for You. This world may
give me no credit for the sacrifices I make for You, but I
know that You see everything that I do. Renew my strength
Father. Help me to finish the race I have started and finish
strong. Let my eyes be fixed on eternity and allow me to
lead others along the way. You are a good, good Father and
I love You will all my heart. Thank You Lord.

Psalm 59:16-17

But I will sing of Your power; Yes, I will sing aloud of Your mercy in the morning; For You have been my defense And refuge in the day of my trouble. To You, O my Strength, I will sing praises; For God is my defense, My God of mercy.

Jesus, let Your name ever be on my lips. I pray that each morning, You are my first thought. I want to praise You each day I awake. Help me to seek You each morning, that I may start every day filled with Your joy. Lord, I never want to forget all of the things that I have to praise You for. For Your great blessings and Your great mercies. You are an amazing God. You are my God. You are my firm foundation, my shelter, my shield, Lord, You are my everything. Help me to run to You in times of trouble. Help me to never take my worries to my friends before I seek Your counsel. God, You are great! You are mighty! Oh, how I love You. Thank You Father for Your never-ending mercies. Be with me this day. Amen.

Psalm 60:11-12

Give us help from trouble, For the help of man is useless. Through God we will do valiantly, For it is He who shall tread down our enemies.

"Give us help from trouble, for the help of man is useless!" Oh Lord, how true it is! Why do we turn to man again and again when it is You alone who is able to save us! God, do not let me pour out my troubles to the ears of men before I have brought them to you. God, they cannot help me like you can. Why do I tend to go there first? Lord, if I am to succeed in this life, it is You who is going to win the battle, it is You who is going to go out and fight for me. Help me to seek Your counsel on all things. Help me to turn to You when I am troubled. Lord, You have surrounded me with wise men and women, but none of them compare to You. Teach me through Your Word, answer my prayers, and deliver me from my times of trouble. Thank You for always hearing me Father. May Your Spirit dwell in me with power. Amen.

Psalm 61:1-2

Hear my cry, O God; Attend to my prayer. From the end of the earth I will cry to You, When my heart is overwhelmed; Lead me to the rock that is higher than I.

Oh Lord, my song shall never change, once again I ask you, "hear my cry, O God." My own wanderings catch me off guard, yet they are as faithful as the sun. I seem to get off track very easily and You allow me to. You give me the freedom to follow You and You give me the freedom to drift away. Well Jesus, my heart is once again overwhelmed, come and save me! I need Your love, I need Your grace, and I need Your arms around me once more. Lead me back into the sweet peace of Your presence. Today I desire to feel the presence of Your Holy Spirit upon me as much as ever before. Use me, O God, for Your purposes. Take my life and let it be Yours. Give me open ears this day to hear Your guidance. Help me to honor You in everything that I do today. Hear my cry Lord, I long for You.

Psalm 62:1-2

Truly my soul silently waits for God; From Him comes my salvation. He only is my rock and my salvation; He is my defense; I shall not be greatly moved.

O God, teach me to wait on You. Teach me to wait long. Teach me to wait frequently and regularly. Lord, this world would have us all rush, but You, O God, have asked us to wait. Teach me to slow down. Teach me to seek You in every moment. Guide me step by step Lord God. I never want to miss a step on Your righteous path. I know that when I rush things that I often make mistakes because of me not waiting on You. Lord, from You alone comes my salvation. To You alone I look for my hope. In You alone I find my help and my trust. Lord You are my one defense. Help me to wait on You.

Psalm 62:8
Trust in Him at all times, you people;
Pour out your heart before Him; God is a refuge for us.

Lord God, You alone know my heart. You alone know my
struggles. I thank You for being a God of great mercy and
great kindness. Help me to trust in You Lord Jesus. Let me
follow You in all of Your ways. Help me to never wander
from the path that You have laid down before me. You are
my refuge! You are my righteousness! Lord Jesus, by Your
blood I have been justified before the Father. I still struggle
at my core to accept that You have freely forgiven me and
that I am perfect in Your eyes. Help me to rest in Your
peace and empower me, by Your Spirit, to live a holy life
that brings honor to Your name Father. I desire to see Your
name be hallowed in all things. Let all the world see that
God is a refuge for His children and that with You on our
side, who can stand against us?

Psalm 63:1-2

O God, You are my God; Early will I seek You; My soul thirsts for You; My flesh longs for You In a dry and thirsty land Where there is no water. So I have looked for You in the sanctuary, To see Your power and Your glory.

Lord, some mornings are hard to rise from bed, but every morning without You feels empty. You are the start of my day and You are the one who sets my course. I do not need more sleep. I need more Jesus. God my soul, how it thirsts for You! My flesh, my whole body, how much it longs for Your presence. Lord, nothing of this world can satisfy the way that You do. Many things bring me a bit of passing pleasure, but only You bring me joy! Only You Lord! How do I wander so often? How am I so easily lured away by the promises of earthly things? Yet when I get there, I find that the well is dry. This world has nothing to offer me that You do not give freely. Every broken road I have gone down has lead me back here, to Your throne, at Your feet. Here in Your presence I feel Your power. I can see Your glory. Lord Jesus, fill me today with Your Holy Spirit. Help me to walk just as You walked because I love You. God, to You I sing praises! You are an awesome God and You have saved me by Your great love. Hallelujah!

Psalm 63:3
Because Your lovingkindness is better than life,
My lips shall praise You.

Lord, let every man, woman, child, and creature, that has breath in their lungs, sing You praise! It cannot come soon enough, the day when every knee will bow and every tongue confess that Jesus is Lord! Father, Your love, Your grace, Your mercies, Your lovingkindness, they all blow me away! I am unworthy to stand before You, but Your Son has washed me clean. God, help me to speak praises today. Help me to stand before fallen men and women and speak praises towards my King. Let me lift my hands in worship and stand unashamed. I do not desire the approval of men. I desire to be satisfied by Your great love alone. Spirit, give me the strength to be a great witness of the gospel. Help me to demonstrate the love that You have shown me. Fill my mouth with praises and gentle words of encouragement. Jesus, make me to be Your hands and feet on this earth. Give me Your heart Lord and let me bring glory to You.

Psalm 63:6-8

When I remember You on my bed, I meditate on You in the night watches. Because You have been my help, Therefore in the shadow of Your wings I will rejoice. My soul follows close behind You; Your right hand upholds me.

Lord, I want You to be the first thing on my mind every morning and I want You to be my last thoughts each night as I lay myself down to sleep. Help me to pray for the people and tasks that You bring to my thoughts as I lay in bed. Help me to surrender my struggles over to You and to seek Your counsel and Your power to see those things through. God, You have never failed me! Not once! So why would You fail me now? Your track record is flawless. Help me to keep my eyes focused on Your flawless past rather than the future which I struggle to hand over to You. Jesus, even while I rejected You, You have always been there for me. You have never abandoned me. You have never left me alone. Therefore, I desire to just rest in Your peace. This night, as I lay myself down to sleep, help me find my greatest rest from You. Amen.

Psalm 64:1

Hear my voice, O God, in my meditation;
Preserve my life from fear of the enemy.

Lord God, You are almighty God, and I know that You hear me when I call. Lord remind me that You hear my cries. That no word or thought goes unanswered. That you keep all my tears in a bottle. You know the hairs on my head by number. God if You know me so well, and have promised to never leave me nor forsake me, help me to not live in paralyzing fear. God help me to live full of Your power and boldness. Father, fight on my behalf so that I know our enemies cannot prevail. Lord, Your Word says, "if God is with us, who can be against us?" Help me to believe that Father. Still my heart and help me to trust in Your amazing power. And when Satan would try to condemn me, help me remember your amazing mercy and grace.

Psalm 64:10

The righteous shall be glad in the LORD, and trust in Him.
And all the upright in heart shall glory.

Lord Jesus, continue to conform me into Your image. Help me to be more like You. Lord, I do not want to miss out on a single one of Your great promises. You promise gladness to the righteous and glory to the upright in heart. Help me to be one of those righteous! Help me to be upright in heart! Father, I want to live my life wholly for You. Help keep me from sin. Control my thoughts. Keep me from temptation. I do not desire to bring shame to Your great name. By the power of Your Spirit working inside of me, I ask you to continue to make me new. Help me to live my life for You and help me to live upright for You. I love You Father. I want You to have my all. Amen.

Psalm 65:2

O You who hear prayer, To You all flesh will come.

Father, I am blown away by Your goodness. I am in awe of Your great love. Words cannot describe the feelings that You give me. God, You hear my prayers! I cannot begin to describe how mind blowing it is that the Lord of heaven and earth listens to me! Like Your servant David said, I am but a flea, who am I? Who am I that the Lord of hosts should look down on me in favor. And yet You do! Lord, I have not earned even one bit of Your love, yet You love me unconditionally. Lord, I pray that all of your children would come to know Your great love and Your peace that surpasses all understanding. You are great Father. You love me so much. Help me to respond to Your great love and live wholeheartedly for You and you alone! Hallelujah Lord, You are good!

Psalm 65:3
Iniquities prevail against me; As for our transgressions,
You will provide atonement for them.

Jesus, You have paid for my sins and You have carried me
further than I could have ever imagined. I am so very
blessed. Forgive me if I ever lose track of just how blessed I
am. You have placed me right where You want me. You
know what I need Lord and You bring those things into my
life, whether I enjoy it or not. You desire growth in me. You
want to draw me closer to You. Lord, continue to pull me in
so that I may dwell in Your house forever! I have tasted the
goodness of Your sweet fellowship. Let me stay close to
You forever. God, when I wander, bring me back quickly.
Correct me quickly Jesus so that I never stray far. All I want
is You Lord. Please be the Lord of my life and let me
continually live for You. Thank You for picking me and
choosing me for the great things You have in store. Thank
You Lord. Bless You.

Psalm 66:12
You have caused men to ride over our heads; We went
through fire and through water; But You brought us out to
rich fulfillment.

Oh Lord, how often do I forget about Your ways? In my
own foolish mind, I sometimes consider myself a finished
product, but You desire so much more from me. Thank You
for reminding me that I am Your child by continuing to
chasten me and put me through trials of refinement. You
don't want my life to be easy Lord, You want it to be
fruitful. Help my heart to receive Your burdens with
gladness. Help me to suppress my moods when I am upset
and let me focus on the eternal picture of what You desire to
accomplish in me. I trust You Father that You desire to
bring me to a place of rich fulfillment. Help me to
remember that You are always at my side. Amen.

Psalm 66:18-20
If I regard iniquity in my heart, The Lord will not hear. But certainly God has heard me; He has attended to the voice of my prayer. Blessed be God, Who has not turned away my prayer, Nor His mercy from me!

Lord Jesus, it has always been Your goodness that draws me to repentance. When will I get to be rid of this body of sin and death? I still stumble in old ways. And the most painful part is feeling separated from You. God, I know that You never leave me. You never forsake me. But I desire to be holy, just as You are holy. Purify me Lord and keep me from sin. For Your name's sake, make me Your humble servant and keep me from all iniquity. Let me hear Your voice again Father. Comfort me with Your Word. I desire to rest in Your presence. You give me such great peace. Peace that this world will never be able to understand. Thank You for hearing my prayers Father. And thank You for never turning Your great mercy from me.

Psalm 67:1-2
God be merciful to us and bless us, And cause His face to shine upon us, That Your way may be known on earth, Your salvation among all nations.

O Holy God! Bless Your children! Pour out Your Spirit upon us and give us holy power to show Your goodness to this earth. We desire to see revival in our lands, in our towns, and in our homes. We desire to see Your law be the law of our land. We want to see hearts longing for You and lives being transformed. Broken families being brought together, shattered lives being reassembled, and our nation to stand strong once again, believing in the promises of Your Holy Word. Shine Your face upon Your people Lord. Burn fierce within our hearts. We want to see Jesus lifted up. Give us boldness to not be ashamed of Your gospel, for it is the power of God unto salvation. Embolden Your people Lord, give us strength to live for You, in Jesus name. Amen.

Psalm 68:19-20

Blessed be the Lord, Who daily loads us with benefits, The God of our salvation! Our God is the God of salvation; And to GOD the Lord belong escapes from death.

LORD God, help me to count my blessings. Father, because of Your Son, Jesus, I have been set free from sin and death. You are so good to me and it is by Your grace alone that I have received so much blessing. As the worries of my day surround me, I pray that I count my abundant blessings. You overwhelm me with grace and goodness. You are so very good to me. You provide for my household, You guide my steps each day, You sanctify me by Your Spirit, and You forgive me all my transgressions. Glory to Your name Father. Let my life bring praises to Your Son Jesus. Help me to count my blessings this day. Let me live in response to Your great faithfulness. Thank You Lord. Thank You.

Psalm 69:13

But as for me, my prayer is to You, O LORD, in the acceptable time; O God, in the multitude of Your mercy, Hear me in the truth of Your salvation.

Lord God, please give me patience! Help me to trust Your great sovereign plan and to wait for the things which You have promised me. I know that You will bring all good things to me in the acceptable time. Let me trust that Your ways are higher than my ways and that You know what is best for me. We see so dimly Lord and cannot tell what the future holds, but You know. Lord Jesus, let me follow in Your footsteps. To pray by faith and to trust in the Father for all things. You know my beginning and my end, You know all my needs, and You know what is best Lord. Help me to trust in You.

Psalm 69:5-6

O God, You know my foolishness; And my sins are not hidden from You. Let not those who wait for You, O Lord GOD of hosts, be ashamed because of me; Let not those who seek You be confounded because of me, O God of Israel.

O God, You know my every sin and struggle. You know the things that still linger within me. And I could never hide them from You. Yet You love me still! Thank You for your mercy and grace Father. Help me never forget that You have forgiven me of all my sins. Help me to never feel condemned. But Lord, please continue Your work of sanctifying me! Help me to become more holy as You are holy. And never let my sins bring down my brothers and my sisters. Help me to never be stumbling block to them. By the power of Your Spirit, help me to control my flesh and my desires. Give me a heart that longs for You all day long. God, You have brought me this far, please uphold me until You return or take me home. Amen

Psalm 70:1

Make haste, O God, to deliver me; make haste to help me, O LORD.

Father God, it is in these lonely times when I wonder why I feel apart from You. I have not heard Your voice for a season and I am ready for that season to be over. I want to feel Your presence move with power within my life. Make haste, O God, and deliver me from my wandering! Deliver me from my own rebellion. Lord, You do not change, nor do You ever leave me. I know that if I feel afar off, it is my own doing. Perhaps You have given me this space for a purpose? I know that You do all things to complete the good work that You have started in me. I trust that You are desiring to see me grow. Lord, I pray that I have endured this season well, but I am ready to have You back again. Come again into my life and show Yourself strong on my behalf. I love You Lord. Amen.

Psalm 70:4

Let all those who seek You rejoice and be glad in You; And let those who love Your salvation say continually, "Let God be magnified!"

Jesus, forgive me if I am ever sad without cause. If I ever feel depressed when I should be thinking about You and Your great salvation. You have saved me, You have redeemed me, all my sins have been justified, and You will one day glorify me in heaven. I really have nothing to complain about. "Let God be magnified!" I pray that the temporary things of this world never overshadow Your greatness, the glory of Your salvation, or the great sacrifice of Your Son. Lord, I let my troubles overwhelm me, but they are nothing in comparison to Your great victory over sin and death. Help me to be filled with Your joy. Help me to rejoice in You always. Let men and women see Your joy within me. Help me to lead them to You with gladness. Restore unto me, the joy of Your salvation, and renew a right spirit within me. Hallelujah Lord.

Psalm 71:1

In You, O LORD, I put my trust;
Let me never be put to shame.

O God, my hope is in You! If You have taught me one thing in all the time that we have walked together, it is to lean not on my own strength and understanding, but to trust in You and Your ways. Lord, if I had gone this far by my own ways, I would be a total loss by now. You have upheld me and carried me at my weakest moments. You have been there for me when I have not been there for You. Lord God, please protect me! Guide me in Your truth! Father, do not let me be put to shame and lead me not into temptation, but Lord, deliver me! For Your Name's sake and for Your glory, keep me from falling! We have come this far, now please Lord, take me further. I want to finish this race strong. I want to enter in to Your kingdom and hear those blessed words, "well done, good and faithful servant." I want to live for You Lord. Please watch over me.

Psalm 71:3
Be my strong refuge, To which I may resort continually;
You have given the commandment to save me, For You are
my rock and my fortress.

O God, let me always turn to You first. Let You and You alone be my shelter. God, help me not vent my sorrows and my troubles to my friends and family before I take them all to You. Help me seek You first in prayer and turn to You first when in need. I know that You can do all things and that through Jesus inside of me, I can face everything that this world can throw my way. Lord your ways are better than my ways. Help me to seek those first. Let me give You the first fruits of my days. Early I will seek You Father. Let the first and last words from my lips be to You each day. As I rise and as I lay, let my eyes be fixed on Your Son. Thank You Jesus for saving me and keeping me. Amen.

Psalm 71:6
By You I have been upheld from birth; You are He who took
me out of my mother's womb. My praise shall be
continually of You.

Lord Jesus, from the beginning of creation You have known me. Before I was conceived You had plans for me. From the womb You protected me. And God, from then until this day You have set me on a path that has led me to right here. God, here I sit before You. At Your feet Father I throw myself. Lord let me stick to Your path. God lead me in Your ways. Help me to trust You with all of my heart and to not lean on my own understanding. You know what is best for me. Let me put all of my trust in Your Holy Word. Daily I must seek it! Rid me of my pride and my slothfulness. Let me never justify a day without seeking You. Help me to place all things into Your hands. LORD God, I surrender.

Psalm 71:8

Let my mouth be filled with Your praise
And with Your glory all the day.

Lord Jesus, give me boldness! Oh that I could speak of You
as I truly desire. God, I falter when I fear the opinions of
others. My pride keeps me from living abandoned for You.
But I want to give You my all Lord. I want to speak freely
of Your goodness, Your mercies, and Your amazing grace.
Loose my lips Father. Let every word that I speak be
seasoned with salt. Let Your praises flow out from my
heart. Let me point people towards You in all that I do. To
You be the glory Father. Lord God, I do not want to be
ashamed of Your gospel. Help me to swallow my fears and
my pride and freely preach the power of God to salvation.
Let me take a stand for Jesus. Give me strength Lord. And
let me give You all of the glory. Amen.

Psalm 71:20

You, who have shown me great and severe troubles, Shall
revive me again, And bring me up again from the depths of
the earth.

Oh Lord, You lift me up and You bring me down. You send
the sun and the rain. Lord God, You give and You take
away. Father, I know that You send me trials to grow me
and to teach me. They teach me to lean on You. They teach
me to trust in Your Word. Lord, I trust that You know best,
but Father, now I pray, revive me again. Let me burn with
zeal and passion. Plant me firmly upon Your Rock and help
me to be bold and strong for Your people. Help me to pray
and act with confidence. Give me the strength I need to
obey even when it is hard. Father, set a fire in my heart once
more and help me point people back to You. Let me be
Your ambassador. Let me be a doer of Your will. I love You
Lord, let me burn for You.

Psalm 72:11
Yea, all kings shall fall down before him:
all nations shall serve him.

Maranatha! Come Lord Jesus come! Father send Your Son
for us. We wait for You patiently. Help us to be blameless
when You come. Do not let me look back to my old life, do
not let me live idly as I wait. Jesus, I pray that You find me
working hard for You when You come. Help me keep my
eyes on Your kingdom and not the things of this earth. Keep
me focused on the salvation of my friends and family,
helping the needy, and seeking the guidance of Your Spirit.
I can't wait until the day that every knee will bow and every
tongue will confess that You are Lord!

Psalm 72:18-19
*Blessed be the LORD God, the God of Israel, who only
doeth wondrous things. And blessed be his glorious name
for ever: and let the whole earth be filled with his glory;
Amen, and Amen.*

God, all that You do is good. All that You do is love. Help
me to learn to trust You in everything that I do. I know that
Your ways are not my ways. My ways tend to be foolish,
but Your ways are good. Everything that You ask of me is
good and everything that You want to give to me is good.
Father, thank you for all of your wondrous gifts. Thank You
for the blessings in my life. Thank You for my family, my
church, and my friends. Thank You for always providing
for me. I long for the day when the whole world will praise
Your great name! Amen

Psalm 73:2 & 23

But as for me, my feet had almost stumbled; My steps had nearly slipped. Nevertheless I am continually with You; You hold me by my right hand.

Oh Lord, you never let me go! I may stumble and even fall, but You lift me back up again. Never let me give in to the lies of the enemy. The lies of condemnation. Lord You loved me long before I ever loved You. You loved me while I was still sinning. Continue to work in me Lord. Conform me into the image of Your Son Jesus. When this world overwhelms me, help me to feel Your presence. God, I long for Your presence in my life. Nothing satisfies like feeling You near. And I know that You never leave me Lord. I am the only one who wanders off. Father, keep me in your loving hands always and continue to guide me down the path that brings glory to Your name. I love You Abba. Hold me and keep me forever.

Psalm 74:1

O God, why have You cast us off forever? Why does Your anger smoke against the sheep of Your pasture?

Father, I know that you never leave my side, but even Your servant David had times of doubt. Help me to hold fast when my faith is weak. Give me the strength to endure when the enemy plants his seeds of doubt. Even when I don't feel Your presence, let me trust in Your Word. I know that Your mercy endures forever and Your promises are unchanging. Keep me in the palm of Your hands Lord. Guide me by Your Holy Spirit. Let my eyes be continually focused on Your Son Jesus. I know You won't leave me or forsake me Lord. Thank You for Your longsuffering and unending kindness. I know You are near and I know that You are here. Amen Abba.

Psalm 74:2

Remember Your congregation, which You have purchased of old, The tribe of Your inheritance, which You have redeemed-- This Mount Zion where You have dwelt.

Before the foundations of the earth were laid, Oh God, You thought of me. Your plans have been from the beginning. You formed me and made me who I am for Your glory. Before I ever took a breath, You committed to send Your Son for me. Even while I was still sinning, You loved me. Lord, thank You that You remain so faithfully committed to me. Help me to show You a similar commitment. God, I desire to give my all to You. You, who has been so faithful and true, deserve more than I could ever give. Lord, I lay down my life for You because You first laid down Your life for me. You have my allegiance, You have my hands and my feet, and Lord, You have my heart. Take this life that I freely give and use it how You see fit. Bless the Lord, oh my soul.

Psalm 75:1

We give thanks to You, O God, we give thanks! For Your wondrous works declare that Your name is near.

Oh Jesus, I do give You thanks! While this life throws a thousand things my way, I should never forget that I am saved! You have set me free from sin and death. Now, let me live this life as one who has been freed by Your great sacrifice. Lord, You make all things new, thank You! Father, You never had to choose me, you never had to offer me anything, but You did it anyway. Thank You! Lord Jesus, I do pray now, all the more, come! Come Lord Jesus and put an end to the pain and suffering on the earth. Let every heart turn to You and let every knee bow. You are an awesome God and I love You. Thank You Lord, thank You.

Psalm 76:11

Make vows to the Lord your God, and pay them; Let all who are around Him bring presents to Him who ought to be feared.

Yahweh God, You are the only One Whom should be worshipped and feared. You deserve all my affection, You deserve all that I have to give. God, I desire to give You my life because it is rightfully Yours. Help me to live in such a way that the fear of man has no bearing on my actions and that I live alone by the fear of God. What can man do to me? God You are for me, who can be against me? You hold the heavens in Your hands, why do I fear what man can do? Father, You alone hold the keys of heaven and hell, why I am ashamed of Your gospel? Lead me Jesus. Show me the way to walk and I will go there. I give You my whole heart and my praise. You alone are worthy of my praise and I will worship You, Yahweh God. Take my life and let it be, consecrated Lord to Thee.

Psalm 77:1-2

I cried out to God with my voice-- To God with my voice; And He gave ear to me. In the day of my trouble I sought the Lord; My hand was stretched out in the night without ceasing; My soul refused to be comforted.

Lord, how often have I found myself apart from You? I alone wander because I know that You are always there. Thank You Lord that You always answer when I call. God, let that not be the only times that I call on You! Lord, I don't want to seek You only when I am in trouble. I don't want to be troubled when I remember You and think about my current estate. I want to think about You and find great peace knowing that I am in the center of Your will. Help me Father, for I am weak. I want to seek You daily! Lord, every hour I need You, so please correct me quickly if I wander from Your path. Like a loving Father, do not let me wander far. Quick and frequent reminders I desire. Do not let me go so far that Your corrections need to be great. But Father, not my will, but Your will be done. I trust that You will teach me through all seasons and trials. But until that day comes, just keep me filled with Your Holy Spirit and the love of Your Son. Amen.

Psalm 78:32
In spite of this they still sinned,
And did not believe in His wondrous works.

Jesus, after all that You have done for us, there are those who still scoff at You and Your great name. You have shown Yourself through Your creation. You have shown Yourself though Your Word. You have shown Yourself through the testimony of Your Spirit and Your Church. Yet there are those who will not turn to You. God, I pray for my fellow man. Lord, they love their wicked ways and they will not repent, they will not turn to You. God, remove the cover from their eyes, remove the grip of the enemy. Help them see the end of their ways and grant them repentance. Lord, I know that You do not desire to see a single man perish, but they choose their evil path. I ask for Your mercy Father. Save them. Help them. Father, use me however You desire to reach the lost. Let them see the error of their ways and let them turn to the only King who ever died for them. Save them Lord, by Your strong hand. Save them.

Psalm 78:4 & 7

We will not hide them from their children, Telling to the generation to come, the praises of the Lord, And His strength and His wonderful works that He has done. That they may set their hope in God, And not forget the works of God, But keep His commandments;

Jesus, let me care for Your children. You have put people in my life whom You desire that I share with and teach Your ways. Let me share Your Word with those who need to hear it. Lord, help me, and my brothers and sisters, to teach our children of Your ways. That they would see our generation as one who loves the Lord our God, who walk in His ways, and who praise Him for all of His goodness. Father, let our lives be a testimony of Your goodness to them. That they may grow up and avoid the foolishness that we entangled ourselves with. I pray that you would bless them and, through us, teach them to walk in Your ways and to keep Your commandments. Lord, may they find their hope in You and You alone. Bless our children Father. Bless our nieces and nephews, our grandchildren, and the children of our friends. Let them be a generation that seeks Your face. And let us be the generation that points them to You.

Psalm 79:13

So we, Your people and sheep of Your pasture, Will give You thanks forever; We will show forth Your praise to all generations.

Oh Lord, let us be a people who are known for singing You praise. That the praises of our Lord would always be on our lips. Jesus, we want to be Your people! We desire to be known as the Jesus people once again! Jesus that our whole existence would be defined by our love for You. Let the people see, let the generations know, that we live for You Lord! Jesus, be our King! Be our Lord! Be our everything! Give me boldness I pray. Overwhelm me with Your presence, to the point where I cannot hold it in. I want You to be the defining characteristic of my life. That I would be known as a worshipper of Yahweh and a follower of Jesus. Holy Spirit, come upon me once again! Fill me with Your presence and Your power. Let me live for You. Amen.

Psalm 79:8-9

Oh, do not remember former iniquities against us! Let Your tender mercies come speedily to meet us, For we have been brought very low. Help us, O God of our salvation, For the glory of Your name; And deliver us, and provide atonement for our sins, For Your name's sake!

Our Father, Who art in heaven, Lord God, hallowed be Your name. Lord God, lead us not into temptation, but deliver us from evil, for Your name's sake. Lord, let all be done, not for my sake Father, but for Your name's sake. God, Your mercies are unending towards me, but not for my sake Father, but because You are good. Let the world know, You are good! And Lord God, deliver me from evil! Keep me from sin! Let me live a life that is defined by love! But not for my sake Father, but for Your great name's sake. Let me never do anything that would bring dishonor to Your name. Lord, I take Your name upon myself. I call myself a Christian, a follower of Christ. Let me not take Your name in vain! Lord God, I want to bring glory to Your name in all that I do. I want my life to be a testimony of Your goodness and Your great love for mankind. Let me live without sin, let me love with abandon, let me give liberally, and let me proclaim Your truths boldly! Yet not for my sake Father, but for Your great name's sake. You are good. Hallelujah.

Psalm 79:10

Why should the nations say, "Where is their God?" Let there be known among the nations in our sight The avenging of the blood of Your servants which has been shed.

Oh Lord, too long You have remained in waiting. Too far Your people have strayed. Show Yourself Lord, strong on behalf of Your people. Rend the heavens and come down once again with revival fire. Let us burn for You once more Oh God. Let the slumbering saints slumber no more and let the prayerless fall to their knees in humility. Stir up the hearts of Your people Lord and give us hearts and eyes fixed upon heaven. Show us Your glory God. Let us glimpse at Your splendor. Revive our tired souls and give us a fervency like when we were first saved. Stop the mouths of the scoffers and open the eyes of the blind Lord. Move with power once more amongst Your people. Help us to long for You Lord. Send us revival. Amen.

Psalm 80:3

Restore us, O God; Cause Your face to shine, And we shall be saved!

God, all we need is You! We struggle through life seeking so many different things, but if You would even give us a glimpse of Your face, all other problems would cease! This is all we need Father, we need to see You. Manifest Yourself to me in my life. LORD God, show Yourself to me in Your Word. Revive my zeal for You and let me burn with fervent heat. Save me from my afflictions and most of all, save me from my sinful self! Only You can do this, Oh God my King. Only You can Save! Lord God, I thank You for Your longsuffering and never ending kindness. And Lord, I now pray, revive Your people! Revive Your Church and let us all burn with zeal. We want to see Your face, O God. We want to see You high and lifted up. Be magnified in my life Father and help me live for You!

Psalm 80:18
Then we will not turn back from You; Revive us,
and we will call upon Your name.

Revive Your people oh God! Send revival to our lands!
Turn the hearts of Your children back to You and have us
call on Your name. Lord, we seek revival! We seek it great
and we seek it small. Lord I desire revival in my own life
first. Come upon me like never before! Set a fire within me
that cannot be contained and let it burn furiously. Father, let
those around the flame which You have kindled and gather
the embers together to create a great fire. Lord, we want our
nation to burn for You once again. Close down the bars, the
pornography industry, and the jails. Let men everywhere
turn to You! Let us all repent and seek You one last time.
That this last revival would be the greatest that this world
has ever seen. Lord, we know You are just, but let this last
revival be so great that when You finally come to take Your
people, that those left behind will have no excuse but to
know that they were left because of their rejection of You.
Revive us again oh Lord. Revive Your people!

Psalm 81:10
I am the Lord your God, Who brought you out of the land of
Egypt; Open your mouth wide, and I will fill it.

LORD God, help me to trust in Your provision! Not just for
the things of this earth, but my spiritual needs, my health,
my strength, and my peace. God, You do not just want to
provide for me, but You desire to fill me. Fill me with Your
Spirit Lord. Fill me with the peace that surpasses
understanding. You are the God who saved me. Now, help
me allow You to be the God who fills me. Allow me to
open up to You. Help me surrender all parts of me to You
so that You can give me the fullest life possible. Never let
me settle for less than Your best God. I know that You have
so much in store for me. Speak Lord, Your servant hears.

Psalm 81:13
Oh, that My people would listen to Me,
That Israel would walk in My ways!

Lord, teach Your children Your ways. So often I see them wondering "where You are" and "why You don't answer", yet they walk in their own ways! They refuse to turn to You, yet they seek You in their times of need. Where are they in the times of plenty Lord? Must we be forced to be in despair before we seek You? God, help us to hear Your voice at all times. Help us to walk in Your ways. Lord, remove the stubbornness in our hearts and give us ears to hear when it is You Who wants to speak to us. God, we want You to be our strong fortress. We want You to fight our battle. Help us to seek You and Your guidance in good times and in bad. Let us always be humbly submitted to Your will, especially when the temptation to do things our way is strong. Lord, I know where my ways have gotten me, and it was not good. Help me trust Your great wisdom and do all things Your way. Help Your children listen to You. To trust in You for all things. Lord, we give it all to You. Lead us Lord, lead us.

Psalm 82:3-4

Defend the poor and fatherless; Do justice to the afflicted and needy. Deliver the poor and needy; Free them from the hand of the wicked.

Lord God, my heart is torn. I see the state of Your children who suffer in the Middle East. I see the countless number of unborn babies who never see the light of day. I see those who are oppressed by slavery and poverty. How long will You allow it to continue? Jesus, I pray for Your return, yet I also see the lost. God there are so many people who have yet to turn to You. God it is hard to watch the suffering in this world, but I also know that You have a plan. Lord, You desire to see all men come to repentance and I trust that You are waiting until every last man has come before You call us home. God, until that day comes, I pray for Your protection. Lord, help those who suffer persecution for Your name's sake. Who face death because of their belief in You. Lord, I trust that every unborn child, that never was able to walk this earth, rests safely with You. God, be near to those who are hurting and are seeking Your face. Comfort the brokenhearted and help me to be Your hands and Your feet until You come. Call upon Your Church to raise up and pursue our calling. Save us Lord. And help us.

Psalm 82:5

They do not know, nor do they understand; They walk about in darkness; All the foundations of the earth are unstable.

Father God, the lost are as blind as can be. They mock You, scoff at Your ways, mistreat Your children, and profane Your holy judgements. Oh Lord, open their eyes. Jesus, show them Your face. Help them to see the end of their ways, for it is only death. Lord, You are not willing that any should perish. You do not find joy in the destruction of the wicked. You desire to see all men be saved and come to the knowledge of the truth. Father help them and use me. As Your Son has said, the laborers are few. Raise up laborers God. Stir the hearts of Your children and revive Your Church to have a heart for lost souls. Lord God, they walk in darkness. Help us to be a light, for You did not save us for us to hide our testimony under a basket. You want us to shine before all men and be a light in the darkness. Help us Lord. Revive us again.

Psalm 83:1

Do not keep silent, O God! Do not hold Your peace And do not be still, O God!

LORD, I know that You see what is going on in the world today. I know You see the laws that are being passed. You see the things that are becoming normal in our society. Lord, the nation is falling quickly, and without Your intervention, I do not know how much longer we can go on like this. Lord God, do not keep silent! Do not withhold Your Spirit Lord. Set Your Church on fire once more and empower Your people for service. Fill our churches and fill Your people. Revive our nation and bring morality back into our homes. Do not be still Oh Lord! Move among us! Oh God, how we need You! And Lord, if You do not choose to revive us, then come. Come Lord Jesus come. Maranatha.

Psalm 83:16

Fill their faces with shame,
That they may seek Your name, O Lord.

Jesus, You died for my friends and family and I pray that
You would help them know that! I do not want to see any
evil thing come upon them Lord, but please, do what You
must to get their attention! Whatever it takes Lord. It hurts
me to think of them facing suffering, but God, help me to
keep my eyes on the eternal. Better they suffer now and be
saved, than suffer forever! God, send whatever You must in
their direction if that is what it will finally take for them to
turn to You. Help them come to a saving faith in You and
let them trust in Your ways. Dear Jesus, save my friends.
Save my family. Do what You must Lord, for their souls'
sake. And keep me in prayer for them. Let their salvation be
in the forefront of my mind continually. Do not let my
friends and family go unprayed for. But Lord, if I don't pray
for them, who else will? If I am the only one whoever prays
for their souls, then let me continue Lord. Keep me in
prayer and keep me seeking Your great mercy. Thank you
for hearing me Lord. Move swiftly.

Psalm 84:1-2

How lovely is Your tabernacle, O Lord of hosts! My soul longs, yes, even faints For the courts of the Lord; My heart and my flesh cry out for the living God. For a day in Your courts is better than a thousand. I would rather be a doorkeeper in the house of my God Than dwell in the tents of wickedness.

Oh Lord. How can I pray more than what has been prayed! How lovely is Your tabernacle! Yes God, my soul does long for You! Lord, it faints within me at the thought of Your great presence. To dwell in Your presence is the greatest joy and pleasure I have ever known. God, all that I am, my heart, my flesh, my soul, they call out to You. You are so good. You love is amazing. Your mercy for me is overwhelming. God Your presence is greater than life. Better is one day in Your courts than a thousand days elsewhere! Yes Lord, I would rather be a homeless man in Your house than the richest man on this earth. God, I pray that You would show this to all who seek You. That they would seek You in holiness, turn from their wicked ways, and enter into the fullness of their Lord. I pray for all who seek you diligently, that they would find You as You have promised. Let Your children feel Your presence. Overwhelm us Lord. We love You!

Psalm 84:6
As they pass through the Valley of Baca, They make it a
spring; The rain also covers it with pools.

Jesus, I love to walk with You on the mountaintops, but I
know that You are also with me in the valleys. Lord, when I
pass through the low places of this life, filled with weeping
and tears, I pray that I have the strength to trust in You.
God, I do struggle to count it all joy when I fall into trials,
but I know that You work much good out of them. I know
that you develop patience within me. Father, help me to
build wells when I enter those valleys. Help me to trust that
You are creating in me things that will bless those who will
enter those valleys after me. I know that You will work all
things to the good in my life. Just help me to remember it
when the times get tough. And I pray, Lord, that I can be a
blessing to those who face similar trials in times to come.
Complete Your good work in me Lord, I trust You.

Psalm 85:6
Will You not revive us again,
That Your people may rejoice in You?

O Lord I pray, revive us again! Revive Your Church! Lord,
I have read of the stories of the days of old. I have seen the
ripple of the great movings of Your Holy Spirit. But alas
Father, my generation has seen no such moving! I want to
see You move Lord! I want to see Your Church on fire with
zeal for You and Your Word. Lord, that we all would turn
from our wicked ways and seek Your face. Help us Lord!
We need Your power more than ever. We need a great
sweeping of revival to come across our land. Lord, we want
to see You move. Father, we long to rejoice in You. Come
quickly, Lord. Come.

Psalm 85:8
I will hear what God the Lord will speak, For He will speak
peace To His people and to His saints; But let them not turn
back to folly.

Lord, I want to pray a prayer of protection around Your
children. My brothers and my sisters. Father, nothing hurts
more than to see a man turn to You and serve You, only to
fall back into his old ways. I cannot believe the brothers and
sisters that I have lost. We once served You together and
when faced with a trial they turned away. It hurts me Father.
To see any of Your children do anything other than to serve
You with all their hearts. God protect us, shield us, and
wrap Your loving arms around us. But I trust You God. I
know that You would not do Your children any harm and
that the things You allow serve Your purposes. No matter
what happens Lord, please give me the strength to stay the
course. To not be moved or shaken. Help me to be there for
my friends and family when they turn back to You. I ask
these things in Your Son's name. In Jesus' name. Amen.

Psalm 86:11
Teach me Your way, O Lord; I will walk in Your truth;
Unite my heart to fear Your name.

Father, You have taken me so far from where I once was.
You have saved me and cleansed me of my sin. Please
Lord, I pray, continue to make me more like Your Son
Jesus. I want to bring glory to Your name in all that I do. I
want to walk in Your ways and live a life that honors You.
Father, give me Your Spirit and unite my heart with Your
heart. Give me Your heart for the lost and Your heart for the
broken. Help me to love like You love and give liberally to
those in need. Help me to have an eternal mindset and not to
be consumed with the things of this life. I want to serve You
with all that I am. Spirit, come upon me once again.

Psalm 86:5

For You, Lord, are good, and ready to forgive, And
abundant in mercy to all those who call upon You.

Lord Jesus, I give You my life and all that I am. I place my
soul in Your hands. Lord, You are so good to me and you
never forsake me. No matter how many times I wander and
stray, You welcome me home. You are always ready to
forgive me my trespasses and You show me so much
mercy. Thank You again Lord. You are a great God and
Your mercy endures forever. And not to me only, but You
are great to all of Your children. All who seek You find
You. Thank You for Your amazing grace and Your
unending love. Bless You Lord.

Psalm 87:7

Both the singers and the players on instruments say,
"All my springs are in you."

Lord God, all of my springs, all of my fountains, every
good thing or good thought that I have is in You. You are
my morning and my night. You are the One who calms the
storms and the One who sets me on the paths of life. God, I
want to find my whole being in You. I want my life to be
defined, not simply by who I am, but by who I am in You.
God, every good thing comes from You. From the sun to
the rain, You have made everything and You pour out
blessings on my life. Thank You for caring for me and
providing for me. Oh God, You are my God, and I will ever
praise You.

Psalm 88:1-2

O Lord, God of my salvation, I have cried out day and night before You. Let my prayer come before You; Incline Your ear to my cry.

Lord, I believe, but help me with my unbelief. So often when I cry out to You, I feel as if You are afar off, but I know that it isn't so. You have told me that You would never leave nor forsake me. I know that You are always by my side, yet sometimes I feel alone. Father God, help me to rebuke these thoughts. I know that you hear and I know that You are near. Never let me forget the great promises of Your Word. I know You hear my cries. I know You can see my broken spirit. Lord, draw me near to You so that I can feel Your presence once again. Never let me drift away as I am prone to do. Help me to meditate on Your promises daily. Lord, I know that You hear my cry. Thank You Lord.

Psalm 88:13

But to You I have cried out, O Lord, And in the morning my prayer comes before You.

Father, this life sends many distractions my way. Whether bills, family, work, or just a lack of sleep, it is always "most convenient" to skip out on my time with You. Help me to put You first Lord. Help me to make You the top priority of my day. God, do not let a morning go by where I do not think of You first. I want You to be the first thought on my mind when I get up and the last person I talk to before I lay to sleep. Be the center of my life Lord Jesus. I want You to be my top priority in my life and in my day. Continue to draw me closer to You. Lord, it is Your goodness that draws me near. Thank You for all that You do for me. Amen.

Psalm 89:1

I will sing of the mercies of the Lord forever; With my mouth will I make known Your faithfulness to all generations.

Lord God, be at the forefront of my mind all the day long. I want my cup to overflow with the praises of my God and my King. Help me to not be ashamed or embarrassed by You. Forgive me for ever being timid about You and Your great works. I want to shine brightly before all men. I desire to be the saltiest salt upon all the earth! I want to live courageously for You! You are my God! You are my king! You have saved me! Help me to live like one of the redeemed, who know where their great deliverance has come from. Let me teach it to my children, to my friends, and to my family. I want to share Your good news with all who will hear. Let me shout it from the rooftops! "Salvation comes through Jesus Christ alone!" Hallelujah!

Psalm 89:6-7

For who in the heavens can be compared to the Lord? Who among the sons of the mighty can be likened to the Lord? God is greatly to be feared in the assembly of the saints, And to be held in reverence by all those around Him.

Oh great and powerful God, You spoke the earth into existence. The stars and the planets were formed at Your command. You hold all things together and one day You will let it all go. The earth will burn with fervent heat and all that is therein. Lord God, there is nothing like You on this earth for us to compare You to. We forget Your power, Your majesty, and Your justice. Lord, I pray that in light of Your amazing grace, I never forget Your justice. Father, in light of You adopting me as Your child, I pray that I never forget that You are the Lord over all creation. God, You are to be feared and referenced. When sin comes to tempt me, remind me of how powerful and mighty of a God it is that I sin against. Every time that I ask for forgiveness, remind me of the great cost that my forgiveness was bought with. Lord, keep me humble before You all of my days. Let me walk circumspectly, redeemed every step of my life, knowing that the all-powerful One has bought me with His own blood. Let me live for You Lord. Amen.

Psalm 90:12
So teach us to number our days,
That we may gain a heart of wisdom.

Lord God, all of our days are numbered, and we live them like we have many years to go, but Lord, Your Word says that our lives are like vapor. One minute we are here and the next we are gone. Help us to be eternally minded Lord! Kingdom minded! Teach us to number our days and live like each one could be our last. I want a heart of wisdom Lord. Do not let the sun set with a pile of unfinished business before me. Let every encounter be treated like it could be my last. Help me to reach my lost friends and family. Do not let me falsely trust in an abundance of time. I want to be proactive Lord. Help me to live for You! Teach me how to be wise with my time and not look back upon a wasted life. My one great desire in life, is to look back on all that I have done, and look ahead to You, saying to me, "Well done, good and faithful servant."

Psalm 90:13
Return, O Lord! How long?
And have compassion on Your servants.

Oh Lord my God, we long to see You move with power yet once more. Before You bring all things to an end, pour out Your Spirit afresh. Revive Your Church Father God. Teach Your children to pray! Break our hearts for the lost! Let us hunger for Your Word! Oh God, how long? Lord, by Your mercies alone, and for Your glory alone, send down revival. Move in such a way that the outside world cannot deny Your presence among Your people. Help us turn our hearts back to You! Show us Your glory. Lord God, we want to see Your face. Father, we look to You alone to be our help, our shield, and our salvation. You've blessed the saints of old God, would you please do it again?

Psalm 90:17

And let the beauty of the Lord our God be upon us, And establish the work of our hands for us; Yes, establish the work of our hands.

Gracious Lord, You are beautiful. I see Your beauty in the sun and in the stars. I see it in the depths of the sea. The lone flower on the high mountain top. The majesty of the unsearched depths of the sea. You are beautiful Lord. God, let Your beauty and majesty be seen in all that I do. Let my works testify of Your goodness. I desire my own works to be reflections of Your Great works. Help me do all things in such a way that it honors You. Let all of my works be a testimony of Your goodness. Let me do all things as unto You Lord. Do not let me slack off as others slack. Let me work hard for Your glory and then You be my rest. Give me deep sleep knowing that I am serving You, my King.

Psalm 91:1

He who dwells in the secret place of the Most High Shall abide under the shadow of the Almighty.

Oh Lord, You're beautiful. In Your presence I find fullness of joy. Oh God, how quickly I can forget. I am the one who walks away from the mirror and forgets what was seen. Day by day I forget just how wonderful Your presence is, but You have remained faithful to show me. Oh Lord, how wonderful You are. What great peace You bring me. I look forward to the day when I can forever remain at Your feet. Beneath the shadow of Your wings. Never to wander again. Never to fear again. Never to leave Your wonderful presence. Oh Lord, haste the day when my faith shall be sight! When we will speak face to face. Oh Lord, haste the day.

Psalm 91:7

A thousand may fall at your side, And ten thousand at your right hand; But it shall not come near you.

Father, of all those who walk the earth, You have chosen me. Unworthy, undeserving, and unappreciative, yet You love me still. God, You have brought me this far and I have learned that You are my only hope to take me the rest of the way home. It pains me to see those who fall away. We once walked side by side, yet they have wandered, strayed, or have fallen prey to the evil one. How have I made it this far? It is You Lord! Let me never put my trust in my own flesh. It is You alone who upholds me. You are my strength and my beacon of hope. You are my Northern Star that guides me in the darkest of nights. You lead me Lord. Thank You for never letting go of me. Lord, I have let go before, but You did not. You held on when my strength was weak and You did not let me fall. Thank You Lord. Your mercy and goodness is forever faithful.

Psalm 91:15

He shall call upon Me, and I will answer him; I will be with him in trouble; I will deliver him and honor him.

Oh Lord Jesus, how I have set my love upon You. I do love You Lord! With all of my heart, I love You, my King. You lead me and guide me, by Your strong Word. You have shown me how to live and how to thrive. Let me rest in Your goodness. Thank You for hearing me when I call Lord. I am humbled before You. That You would look upon me with such great love. God, You are always here for me. Thank You. You deliver me from all of my enemies and struggles. Thank You. All that I have, You have given me. Thank You. And Lord, above all, while I was still sinning against You, You saved me. Thank You so much for Your goodness, Your kindness, Your mercy, and Your grace.

Psalm 92:1-2

It is good to give thanks to the Lord, And to sing praises to Your name, O Most High; To declare Your lovingkindness in the morning, And Your faithfulness every night,

Oh God, if only I gave You the praise that You deserve. I would praise You with every breath that You have given me. Father, help me to give You the praise that You are due. Lord, if it were my way I would wake every morning with Your praises on my lips. You would be my heart's prayer as I lay myself to sleep. As I sit to eat or rise up to work, You would be on my heart and on my lips. You are worthy of my praise Lord. You are wonderful. You are so gracious and loving. You show mercy to the undeserving and You show no partiality in Your righteous judgment. Oh Lord, You are altogether good. One day the earth will be full of Your praises. One day all people will shout. Worthy is the Lamb! Worthy is He of all glory and praise! And holy, holy, holy is the Lord God Almighty. Lord, let Your people shout. Amen.

Psalm 92:5

O Lord, how great are Your works! Your thoughts are very deep.

Lord, You blow me away! Every time You meet with me, You blow me away. How will I ever discover the depths of Your great love? Your Word is continually being opened to me. Again and again I consume it, yet there is always more to be found. God, the majesty of Your Word is unending. Like the baskets of bread and fish that fed the multitudes, Your Word never ceases to provide for me. I eat until I am full and there is always more to spare. How do the scoffers not see? How can they doubt the supernatural inspiration of Your Holy Word? God, unveil their eyes and help them see their foolish ways. That they too can know the depths of your knowledge and wisdom.

Psalm 92:6

A senseless man does not know,
Nor does a fool understand this.

LORD God, the wicked do not know You. The foolish live without You. They do not see the end of their ways. They do not fathom that they will one day reap what they have sown unless they turn from their ways and seek Your face. Father, it can be so frustrating trying to show them the end of their ways; trying to show them their need for Your salvation. God, never let my heart grow hard. No matter how wicked the sinner Lord, do not let me become callous, for You saved even me. Like small children, they run and are unaware. They just do not see. Lord, please open their eyes. Open the eyes of the blind Lord! Send down Your Spirit and show Yourself to sinful man. They are so lost Lord, yet so too was I. Never let me forget, never let me give up, and help me to keep my eyes on You.

Psalm 93:4

The Lord on high is mightier Than the noise of many
waters, Than the mighty waves of the sea.

Lord, though the seas rage and the rains fall, You are mightier still! Though the world clamors in fear, You are still on the throne. LORD God, keep our eyes on You in these troubled times. Remind us that You are from everlasting to everlasting. You knew all of this would come before You laid the foundations of the earth. You knew where I would be this day. Father God, comfort Your people. Remind us to pray. Show us Your power and glory at work in our lives. Help us to turn to You in troubled times. Help us to seek Your face. In all that we do, let us give honor and glory to You Father God. Oh Lord, You are on the throne. Remind me that You are on the throne. Though the floodwaters raise up, and they lift their voice, You are on the throne. Forever and ever, amen.

Psalm 93:5

Your testimonies are very sure; Holiness adorns Your house, O Lord, forever.

God, You have never failed. You have told us the future before it has happened. You have revealed to us Your creation and it has testified of Your power. God, all that You do is wholly good. For You are all powerful and You are holy. God, since we have so many great witnesses of Your faithfulness, help us never to doubt You. Help us trust that, as You have always come through before, You will continue to do so. I can trust every promise that You have ever made to me because You cannot lie. You cannot change. And You cannot fail! God, let me trust You always. Let me put all of my faith and hope in You. Jesus, You are unstoppable!

Psalm 94:14

For the Lord will not cast off His people, Nor will He forsake His inheritance.

Lord, no matter what I do, no matter how far I stray, it amazes me that You would never leave me. You would never abandon me. I know I don't deserve such great faithfulness and it only reminds me that it is only by Your grace. Thank You for always being with me. Thank You for being so faithful when I feel empty. I love You God. You are amazing and Your mercy endures forever. Help me show even a fraction of Your unending love to those around me today. Help me to be there for them when they don't deserve it. Give me the strength to love them as You have loved me. Thank You Father.

Psalm 94:17

Unless the Lord had been my help, My soul would soon have settled in silence.

What if Lord? What if You had not been there for me? What if I had never found You? Oh Lord, where would I be today if it wasn't for Your mercy? God You have saved me from sin and You have saved me from myself! God, without Your strong hand to guide me, I do not know where I would be today. Thank You for sending me down Your path. Lord, I pray You keep me on that path and do not let me veer far. I do not want to go back to my old ways and my old self. I want to live my life entirely abandoned unto You. God, I once walked according to my own heart, but now I walk according to Your heart that You have put inside of me. Thank You for the guidance of Your Holy Spirit. May He guide me always.

Psalm 94:19

In the multitude of my anxieties within me, Your comforts delight my soul.

Lord God, I can tell when I begin to lose sight of You. My anxieties begin to fester. Lord, You bring me such great comfort and peace. When I know that everything is in Your hands, I can face all that this world throws my way. But when I lose sight of You, Your power, Your sovereign hand, I begin to do things in my own strength. And when I take things upon myself, I begin to feel the stresses of success and failure. I worry. I plan and I strive. And the world begins to come crashing in, until I hear Your still small voice. You tell me to cast my cares upon You. You tell me to take all things to You in prayer. You tell me to trust You, that You will work all things to the good. God, Your comforts delight my soul. Thank You.

Psalm 95:6-7

Oh come, let us worship and bow down; Let us kneel before the Lord our Maker. For He is our God, And we are the people of His pasture, And the sheep of His hand.

Oh God, You are wonderful. You are amazing. You are simply and wondrously good. Help me to live my life at Your feet. Seeking Your face all day long. God You made the heavens, You made the oceans, and You made me. How wondrous You are! Oh Lord, let me simply be one of Your sheep. Let me always be listening to the call of my Great Shepherd. Let Your rod correct me and Your staff guide me. Let me dwell in Your goodness always. Help me, this day, to just rejoice that I am Yours. God, and that You are mine. Hallelujah Lord.

Psalm 95:7-8

Today, if you will hear His voice: "Do not harden your hearts, as in the rebellion, As in the day of trial in the wilderness,"

God, help me to hear Your voice. Do not let me become engaged in things that deafen me to Your guidance. Do not let me become distracted by things that would overshadow Your place in my life. Father, give me a heart that rejoices in Your ways. I don't want to fight them. I don't want to turn from them. Lord, I want to enter into Your rest! I want to experience the fullness of what You promise Your children. Help me to live my life under the shadow of Your wings and let me never depart from Your ways. Let Your Word guide me in all that I do. And Lord, help me trust that as I place all things into Your hands, that You will take care of them, and that I can rest assured that the Lord of the universe has everything under control. Amen Lord.

Psalm 96:2

Sing to the Lord, bless His name; Proclaim the good news of His salvation from day to day.

Lord, right here in Your Word it tells me to "Proclaim the good news of Your salvation from day to day." God, give me the courage to truly share your gospel from day to day. That every day as I lay to sleep, I can look back and think upon how I was pointing people to You. I want to be rid of the fears I have and the hesitation I have in sharing Your love with those around me. I just want to be open with everyone I meet that You are my God and that I love You with all my heart. Jesus, You are the answer to this world's problems. You are the healing that these sick people need. Help me to share Your healing. Help me to share Your love. Let me live out the Great Commission from "day to day".

Psalm 96:13

For He is coming, for He is coming to judge the earth. He shall judge the world with righteousness, And the peoples with His truth.

Jesus, You are coming soon! Let Your coming put a swiftness in my step. Help me to be surrendered to Your will minute by minute. Help me be strong when I feel weak. Jesus, You are coming! Let me not be ashamed of Your gospel. Give my lips words to speak to those who are perishing around me. Help me touch the lives of my family who are still lost without You. Jesus, You are coming! Lord, give strength to my brothers and sisters who are being persecuted. Help them to stand fast, even when threatened by death, not to renounce Your great name. Give them a hope for tomorrow. Jesus, You are coming! One day I will stand before You. At Your feet I will give an account for every deed I have worked on this earth. Lord, correct me when I waver and direct me down Your paths. The time is short. There are still lost who need to be saved by Your amazing grace. Use me Lord Jesus. You are coming!

Psalm 96:3

Declare His glory among the nations,
His wonders among all peoples.

Holy Spirit, I pray that You live boldly inside me today. I pray that I will look for every opportunity to declare Your great works. Friends, family, classmates, and coworkers need to hear about who you are! Lord, You are amazing and I love You! This world looks for satisfaction in all the wrong places. Help them Lord. Help them see that they are serving pathetic idols and that You are the One True King. God, You made the heavens and the earth! How small are my needs compared to Your great works? Help me to keep my eyes on Your throne and on Your strength and beauty. Lord, bless me and keep me, and make Your face shine upon me. Amen.

Psalm 97:1

The Lord reigns; Let the earth rejoice;
Let the multitude of isles be glad!

Oh Lord my God, when darkness surrounds me and disappointments come, let me never forget that You are on the throne! You God, have reigned, do reign, and will reign forever. You are still the sovereign God of this earth. Father, help me to look at this day through eternal lenses. Let me see all things as part of Your perfect plan. Help me to be always rejoicing that my King will reign forever. You are awesome and glorious God. I thank You that You have called me Your own. I rejoice that my God reigns.

Psalm 97:10

You who love the Lord, hate evil! He preserves the souls of His saints; He delivers them out of the hand of the wicked.

LORD God, every day as I reflect, I realize how far I fall from Your majesty. You are holy and true. Lord, I desire to please You and I ask for Your strength to be upon me. Father, help me to hate sin! Not only do I want to be free from my sins, but I want to hate it as You do. I want to hate evil things and not merely avoid them. Give me boldness to speak out, give me strength to cast it far from me, and give me an aching heart for those who are still entangled by it. Like a dog returning to its vomit, I too get lured by my old ways and habits. My spirit wrestles with my flesh. Help me to be done with it all Lord! Help me to live pure and holy for You! And Lord Jesus, let me never forget that I am preserved and forgiven because of what You did for me. You have saved me. Thank You Lord. Thank You!

Psalm 98:4

Shout joyfully to the Lord, all the earth; Break forth in song, rejoice, and sing praises.

Lord God, help me to always be singing Your praises! This world is filled of people with woes and complaints, Help Your children to bring light to this hurting world. Let Your Word be a song on our lips all day long. Let us show joy to those who are lost around us. Help us to shout and sing of all the great things You have done. Help us to long for You. Help us to long for fellowshipping with one another. The enemy comes to divide, but You Lord, You come to unite us. Unite our song Father. Let us sing to You with one voice. Hallelujah Lord! We love You!

Psalm 98:9

For He is coming to judge the earth. With righteousness He shall judge the world, And the peoples with equity.

Father God, Your ways are so much higher than mine. I do not know, nor will I ever understand, how You judge. But I know that You are good. I know that You are fair. Lord, You will judge this whole earth with equity. One day, every knee will bow before You and every tongue will affirm that Your ways are good and true. And while we look through a glass dimly, I pray that my faith holds and I never doubt Your goodness. For one day You will reveal all Your ways to me and I shall see. But until that day, I will walk by faith. God Your Word is a light unto my path and a lamp unto my feet. Help me trust in Your holy Word with all of my heart, mind, soul, and strength. Grow me in Your Word Father, that I might know You and Your Son more. You are so, so, good Lord. I love You.

Psalm 99:6

Moses and Aaron were among His priests, And Samuel was among those who called upon His name; They called upon the Lord, and He answered them.

God, never once have You forsaken me. Never once have You let me down. Never once have You not come through on Your promises. So then why do I doubt You now? Why do I ever worry? Why do I ever question the outcome of my trials? God, all who have ever called on Your name, You have answered them. You have promised that all who diligently seek Your face will find You. Time and time again we fail Lord, but not You! God, we wander and stray, yet You find us and remind us that You are the God who forgives! How can a holy God forgive such unholy people? It is Your love Lord. That You love us so much, You sent Your Son to die for us. What amazing love! Help me to live in Your love Lord. Let it give me peace in all of my troubles. Help me to forever remain in Your presence.

Psalm 100:3
Know that the Lord, He is God; It is He who has made us, and not we ourselves; We are His people and the sheep of His pasture.

Lord Jesus, You have bought me at a price, the price of Your blood. So often I forget that I am not my own. God, this life is not about me! It is about You! You are my great Shepherd and I am but a sheep in Your flock. Help me not to wander and stray and lead me back again when I do. Lord, let my desires be aligned with Your desires. Take out my heart of stone and put in Your heart Lord. I want my heart to break for what breaks Yours! I want to rejoice in those things which You rejoice in. God, I thank You for all that You have done. All that I own is from You. All whom I love are from You. You have never put me through anything without consideration. I am where You have placed me. Now help me to live this life for You! Give me strength when I am weary to keep on fighting this battle. Help me defeat my foes through love. Help me to show them love, just like You showed me love while I was an enemy to You. Oh God, You truly are amazing. Overwhelm me Lord!

Psalm 101:3-4

I will set nothing wicked before my eyes; I hate the work of those who fall away; It shall not cling to me. A perverse heart shall depart from me; I will not know wickedness.

Lord God, convict me! Lord, I have no desire to be a part of what You call evil. Convict me Lord! If I am being slack, if I am being permissive, if I am taking pleasure from what You despise, convict me! Lord, my heart is often callous to Your ways and this world throws sinful pleasures at me all day long. Whether lustful, obscene, coarse, and just simply unedifying, I find myself drawn away by them. Help me to not take lightly what You take seriously. Do not let me support these industries of wickedness. Let my house forever be a place where You are worshipped. Help me to take a stand when no one else will!
Lord, I do not want a perverse heart. I have no desire to pleasure in wickedness. Let me weigh out my choices and count the cost of my pastimes. May Your love and Your grace be with me, now and always. And may I stay, blameless until You come. Amen.

Psalm 102:1-2

Hear my prayer, O Lord, And let my cry come to You. Do not hide Your face from me in the day of my trouble; Incline Your ear to me; In the day that I call, answer me speedily.

Lord God, I pray that You hear me. Though I know that You are always there, I often struggle with doubts. You never forsake me Lord, yet I often feel alone. It isn't You who wanders Father, it is me. I wander and stray. I often become distracted by the things of this world and I lose track of You. But God, here I am! Help me to return to You quickly. I want to follow You all of my days! Let me see You move in my life once again. Help me to be strong on Your behalf. Lord, may Your grace and love be upon me. Keep me from temptation, keep me from wandering, and keep me from sin. Embrace me with Your loving arms and never let me go. I love You Father. Maranatha.

Psalm 102:12
But You, O Lord, shall endure forever, And the remembrance of Your name to all generations.

Great is Your faithfulness Lord God Almighty! Since You laid the first stone of creation and until the last is devoured, You have remained the same and You will continue to on into eternity. Lord, this world is full of changes, and we as people are not usually excited of change, but You never change Lord. While my friends may waver and falter, You never change! While the seasons come and the seasons go, You are constant! While my life is often filled with so many uncertainties, You remain the same! Thank You Lord for never changing. It gives me so much peace to know that You will never back out on me or change the rules on me. You are the Almighty, the unchanging God. Thank You for never changing and thank You for remaining faithful to a feeble believer like me.

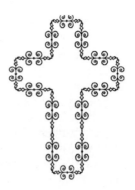

Psalm 103:11-12

For as the heavens are high above the earth, So great is His mercy toward those who fear Him; As far as the east is from the west, So far has He removed our transgressions from us.

Lord Jesus, you ways are so good and so true and I feel as if I will never be able to wrap my mind around them. And above all else, Your forgiveness blows my mind. I cannot earn it and I cannot understand it, but You have taken my sins from me. I never feel like I can thank You enough, but You did it because You wanted to. You saved me because of Your goodness, not mine. Your mercy is beyond comprehension and Your grace is without measure. You have removed my sins further than the mind can know. Lord, I may never fully understand how You could have died for a sinner like me, but let me live my life in response to that. Help me serve You! Help me follow You! Your grace is amazing!

Psalm 103:13-14

As a father pities his children, So the Lord pities those who fear Him. For He knows our frame; He remembers that we are dust.

You are a good, good Father! You love us so much. And You treat us as we ought to be treated. As helpless toddlers. God, I know that my greatest achievements are like a toddler's somersaults in Your eyes. I may look silly, but You smile and You encourage me to keep going. You always push me forward and You never beat me down. You know just how much I can handle and You push me to my limits. You are always trying to help me grow. And when I become foolish and full of pride, You gently remind me that I am but dust. None of us will ever be as good of a parent as You are, but once again, You model perfection for us. God, help me to show this same tender love to those around me. There are no people like me, Lord. There are only those who are ahead and those who are behind. Help me to learn from those who are ahead and help me to lead and love those who are behind. You are a good Father Lord, and I love You.

Psalm 103:1
Bless the Lord, O my soul;
And all that is within me, bless His holy name!

O Lord, thank you for all that You do and all that You've done! I do not thank You nearly enough. For You have done amazing things on behalf of me and Your people, but we often forget to give You the praises You deserve. Lord You heal and You forgive and You cleanse! Even the littlest of joys in my life all come from You. Though my health may not be perfect, You have given me this day and I desire to praise You with it. Help me to live as an act of praise for You my King. Jesus, let Your name be on my lips and help me to boast of You to the peoples. You are my King and I love You! Hallelujah!

Psalm 103:17
But the mercy of the Lord is from everlasting to everlasting
On those who fear Him, And His righteousness to children's
children, To such as keep His covenant, And to those who
remember His commandments to do them.

Lord God, be with my family forever. Help me to stay true to Your Word and to keep Your commands so that my family can see You working in me and will likewise follow. I desire for You to be the God of my house. To rule and reign over my family. Help us to speak of You as we rise up and as we lay down. Be the center of our conversations and be the focus of our visions. Lord, let Your mercy be over our house for as long as we seek Your face. And when we stay, remember us, and bring us back to You. Lord, be quick to correct us if we wander. Do not let us go far! Keep us by Your side and help us to lead others to You. Let the LORD be the God of our house for generations to come. Amen.

Psalm 103:8 & 10

The Lord is merciful and gracious, Slow to anger, and abounding in mercy. He has not dealt with us according to our sins, Nor punished us according to our iniquities.

Father You are so merciful. You know me better than I know myself and I just cannot understand how You continue to be so gracious with me. Lord, I am like a rebellious child at times, and other times worse! I kick and I scream when I do not get my way, though nobody else around me knows it. This world does not know the depths of my struggles and my temptations, but You know. I can hide nothing from You, yet You love me still. You know my secret failures and my hidden failures, yet You bear with me. Lord, I know that You will not deal so graciously with Your creation, and I pray that those who don't know You now will come to know You soon before that day comes.

Psalm 104:6-7

You covered it with the deep as with a garment; The waters stood above the mountains. At Your rebuke they fled; At the voice of Your thunder they hastened away.

LORD God, You are very great and the whole world is Yours! You made it, You have already once judged it, and You will judge it again! Lord, You foresaw that the day was coming, and it is now here, where people mock Your creation. They do not believe that You created from nothing, they do not believe that You flooded Your creation. Yet all of creation testifies of You! Help them to see the beauty of Your majesty. Help the lost to see the care and thought You have put into the tiniest details of life. The beauty of a flower, deep in the forest where no man will see. The majesty of the cosmos where no man can go. From the ant to the mountain, they declare Your great power. Lord, unveil the eyes of my nation. Help them to turn to You once more.

Psalm 104:10

He sends the springs into the valleys,
They flow among the hills.

Oh Lord my God, You alone send springs into the valleys.
And Lord, I am yet again in a valley. Without You it would
be so dry. Without You it would be so barren. Yet You send
me springs. You give me water to drink when I ask for it.
You sustain me in a land that is unbearable. Help me to trust
that the springs will keep coming. Help me to look to the far
off hills from which they come. I know that the valley will
not go on forever Lord, but while I am here, help me to trust
in You. Help me to depend on Your springs, Your Living
Water. You sustain me Lord. Let not my eyes seek after
other things. To You alone do I look and in You alone do I
trust. Send the springs Lord, Your servant is thirsty.

Psalm 104:33-34

I will sing to the Lord as long as I live; I will sing praise to
my God while I have my being. May my meditation be sweet
to Him; I will be glad in the Lord.

God, I pray that all of my prayers are a blessing to You.
Like a child to his parent, I pray that You are overjoyed by
my love for You. I want to sing to You forever. You have
my heart. You have saved my soul. And now, Lord, I just
want to live my life for You. I just want to make You proud
of me and my love for You. I desire nothing more in this
life than to know that I will someday enter into Your
presence and You will tell me, "well done." God, You are
so, so good and I love You. With all my heart, I love You!
Thank You for all that You have done in me and for me.
And not because I am worthy or have earned Your great
love, but simply because You are love and You are merciful
and compassionate. Thank You for being a God who loves!
Thank You for being a God who saves! You are my God
and I will ever praise You!

Psalm 105:1

Oh, give thanks to the Lord! Call upon His name; Make known His deeds among the peoples!

Oh LORD, my God, help me with these three things. Father, help me to give You thanks for all that You have done. So often I come to You in need, in want, and desperate for Your provision, but You deserve my thanks. Remind me to thank You often for all the good You have done and simply for who You are. Yet again Father, help me to call on Your name when I am in need. So often I attempt to take on this world's struggles on my own. I look for every practical way to solve my problems before I turn to You. Help me to seek You first. And Lord, most of all, help me to be a witness of what You have done in my life and what You have done for all mankind. Holy Spirit, empower me to be a witness of the Lord Jesus. Help me to share the gospel with a dying world! Light a fire within my heart that burns with zeal for You Jesus. Let me bring You the honor and praise You deserve.

Psalm 106:3

Blessed are those who keep justice, And he who does righteousness at all times!

Lord Jesus, You were tempted in all things, and knew no sin. You know my struggles. You know my weaknesses. Lord, I ask You to keep me strong when I feel weak. Help me to overcome this world as You overcame it. With Your Spirit within me, I know that I can face all things. Lord, keep me blameless until You come. Let Your love and Your grace flow from me. Lord, let Your name be highly esteemed by the life that I live. I do not want to bring shame to Your name. Watch over me, lest I stumble. Empower me, lest I become weak. Lord feed me, lest I wander in hunger. God, for Your sake, not my own, I ask that You provide for me and my family To show this world that You are great, and to keep us from falling into temptation. Show Yourself strong on our behalf. And watch over us and keep us blameless until You come. Amen.

Psalm 106:30

Then Phinehas stood up and intervened,
And the plague was stopped.

LORD God, give me strength and boldness to stand up for righteousness. Give me words to speak in times of trouble that I might turn people back to You. Father, do not let my lips remain closed when I see wickedness. Help me to take a stand for You and Your Word. Help me to teach the lost of Your commands. Help me to be used to turn back the people to seek You. Again Lord, give me boldness! Help me to not be ashamed of Your gospel! Help me to not let my fears of rejection prevent me from being used to save a lost and dying world! Help me to speak Your Word boldly and without fear! I want to serve You with all that I have. Holy Spirit fall! Come upon me and use me as You wish. I am humbly and forever Yours.

Psalm 106:34-35

They did not destroy the peoples, Concerning whom the
Lord had commanded them, But they mingled with the
Gentiles And learned their works;

God, my spirit is willing, but so often my flesh is weak. Lord, You know my heart. You know that I desire to serve You and You alone. Why do I so often wander and stumble? Lord, Your ways are good and I know that You work all these things to the good as long as I keep on loving You. Jesus, help me to live in this world, but not be tainted by this word, just as You did. Lord, You were tempted in all things, yet never tempted. Holy Spirit, please, continually be whispering in my ear to keep me from sin. Do not let me mingle with the temptations that this world has to offer. Keep me from the knowledge of sin and naive to the wickedness of this world. Help me to walk blamelessly before You all of the days of my life.

Psalm 107:8-9

Oh, that men would give thanks to the Lord for His goodness, And for His wonderful works to the children of men! For He satisfies the longing soul, And fills the hungry soul with goodness.

Lord Jesus, help this world know that You are the answer! You are the answer for our hurt! You are the answer for our pain! Lord we suffer in vain because we do not turn to You. Lord, one day we will all worship You together, but not yet. So many people mock You and turn from You. But Your works are wonderful, Your love is amazing, and Your beauty divine! Lord You fill our souls with goodness, help the people see. You satisfy our soul's longing, help the people see. Turn their hearts back to You Father, unveil their eyes! Stir their hearts by Your Spirit, that they may come to know You while there is still time. Send revival Lord, Your people need You.

Psalm 108:12

Give us help from trouble, For the help of man is useless.

Lord, why do I ask my friends for help? Why do I seek counsel? Why do I turn to books and worldly wisdom when You offer me so much more? God, help me to seek You first! Help me to lay all of my burdens at Your feet before I take them before my brothers. I want You to be my refuge and my first place of turning. I want to quickly be drawn to Your strength and wisdom in my times of need. Thank You Lord for the wise friends You have placed around me, but let me never look to them before You and Your Word. God, in Your Word You have given us all things that we need. Help me seek my answers from You before I seek them from men. Your ways are so much higher than our ways. Lead me down Your path Father, I know that it will be good.

Psalm 108:1

O God, my heart is steadfast; I will sing and give praise,
even with my glory.

Oh Lord, You are amazing and I just want to praise You
this day. So often I come in need, so often I am asking You
for things, but today I praise You. You have given me more
than I could ever need. You have given me the air in my
lungs and You have given me Your Spirit to guide me.
Your Son Jesus has washed away my sin and Your Word
guides my ways. God, Your commandments are good, they
keep me from trouble and pain. Lord, Your sun warms me
and your wind refreshes me. The heavens declare how
amazing You are and the beauty of the flowers show Your
care for us. Help me just praise You this day before all
mankind. For You are good!

Psalm 109:4

In return for my love they are my accusers,
But I give myself to prayer.

Lord, let me live by the words of Your Son. Help me to turn
the other cheek, help me to give without wanting anything
in return, and help me to love those who hate me. Lord, if
they still hate me after I have shown them Your love
through me, let me take it to prayer. Those whom I would
want to hate, help me to pray for them. Those whom I
would want to see fall, help me to pray for them. God, help
me to pray for all mankind alike. Help me to lift up the
wicked before You, that You might change their ways. Let
me pray without hypocrisy, because I know how far You
have taken me. Thank You Lord for all You have done.
You are good!

Psalm 109:26-27
Help me, O Lord my God! Oh, save me according to Your mercy, That they may know that this is Your hand-- That You, Lord, have done it!

Father God, keep me in Your will. Help me to walk along Your paths. Let me not turn aside to the left or to the right. I look to You and Your strength to save me because of myself I have nothing to give. And what I could give would bring You no glory. Let the world see that it is You alone that sustains me. I have no strength left. You must fight for me so the world can see that You are a God that fights on behalf of His people. It is Your grace alone that sustains us. Your mercy is all I hope in. I pray that I never give the appearance of being self sufficient. Let all who see me know that it is You alone who has saved me, You alone who works in me, and You alone who keeps me, day by day. Praise You Lord.

Psalm 110:5
The Lord is at Your right hand;
He shall execute kings in the day of His wrath.

Lord Jesus You are coming back soon! Help me look to You as my Blessed Hope. When the trials and tribulations of this world surround me, help me keep my eyes on my King. Lord, so many people do wrong, but You will one day judge. Take away my own heart of judgement. I don't want to be caught up with thoughts of revenge. Lord, vengeance belongs to You and You alone, and You will judge all my oppressors and Your blasphemers someday. But Father, until that day comes, help me to show them Your love. Help me to live as You have asked me to, in order that I might win their souls back to You. Help me to love unconditionally and to lay my own life down as You laid Your life down for me. I love You Abba! Thank You for Your grace.

Psalm 111:1

Praise the Lord! I will praise the Lord with my whole heart,
In the assembly of the upright and in the congregation.

Take my heart Lord! Make it Yours! God, I want to give
You all that I am. I want You to rule on the throne in my
heart. Let me not share it with any other but You. I want
You to be the king in my life. I want all others to see who I
serve. Father, put Your heart into Your people. Let us long
to see Your kingdom come and Your will be done. This
world has so many temptations that try to draw me away,
but I will keep my eyes on You Lord. You are where I draw
my strength from. You are where I find my refuge. Let me
never find peace in the arms of another. Let me only ever
look to You, my God and my King.

Psalm 111:10

The fear of the Lord is the beginning of wisdom; A good
understanding have all those who do His commandments.
His praise endures forever.

Lord God, help me to love Your Word and Your
commandments. I desire to trust You with all my heart. I
know that Your ways are above my ways and that I will
never fully understand Your ways. Help me to trust You.
When the world is falling down around me and my life
appears to be in shambles, help me to trust You and help me
to reverence You. You are my Father! Help me to have a
godly fear of You. I know that You are good and true, but
You also hate sin and are righteous and holy. God, let me
never feel separated from You, so that I lose focus of Your
great love for me, but never let me become so relaxed with
You that I forget of Your great and powerful holiness. Let
me walk in the wisdom of Your Word all the days of my
life.

Psalm 112:5

A good man deals graciously and lends;
He will guide his affairs with discretion.

Lord Jesus, because of the great sacrifice You have made for me, I am allowed to live free. I am free from sin and free from death. God, You gave Your Son freely to me. Help me to now freely give to others. Help me to hold on to my blessings loosely and be quick to use them to bless others. This world is greedy and has corrupted me with its greedy ways. Help me to give liberally and with joy. And in all this Father, give me great wisdom when dealing with finances and worldly things. Help me know when to spend and when to save. Do not let me squander the great gifts You have given me. I desire to be wise with what You have given me and I want people to know that all good things that I have come from You. You are the source and sole provider of my blessings. You have given me grace upon grace and I thank You for it Lord. Hallelujah, blessed be Your great Name.

Psalm 112:7-8

He will not be afraid of evil tidings; His heart is steadfast,
trusting in the Lord. His heart is established; He will not be
afraid, Until he sees his desire upon his enemies.

LORD God Almighty, help me to fear You! For if I fear You alone, I will fear nothing else. When I have my God on my side, nothing can stand against me. God, when I am living for You, You are looking out for me. Why do I ever question? Why do I ever doubt? You are so good, and faithful, and true. When I keep my eyes fixed upon You I can handle any situation and face any trouble. Why should I fear or doubt? The LORD God is on my side. Whom shall I fear if He is with me? Lord, let this mind be in me at all times! You work all things to my good. You prepare all things to conform me into the image of Your Son Jesus. Help me to always trust Your plan. Your ways are good and far above my comprehension. Lord, if I fear You alone, I will never have a reason to be afraid. If I trust in You alone, I will never be let down. Lead me God and help me to walk in Your ways. Amen.

Psalm 113:1-3

Praise the Lord! Praise, O servants of the Lord, Praise the name of the Lord! Blessed be the name of the Lord From this time forth and forevermore! From the rising of the sun to its going down The Lord's name is to be praised.

Hallelujah Jesus, great is Your Name. Jesus, You are the one that saved me. Jesus, You are the one who upholds me. And Jesus, You are the one who will someday glorify my body to be with You. Praise be to Your name! Let all the world hear and know that Jesus is the name above all names. That You, King Jesus, are the only one who can end the hurt, the pain, and the suffering. It is You, Christ Jesus, whom Your Father had set aside from the dawn of creation to die on the cross for my sin. Praise You Jesus! You have left Your Spirit to love and to guide me. Thank You Lord Jesus! Jesus, let Your name remain forever on my lips. Let all who see and know me, know that I worship the one true God, the Almighty, the Creator, the Lord of my heart, King Jesus. Messiah. Lord.

Psalm 114:7

Tremble, O earth, at the presence of the Lord, At the presence of the God of Jacob,

Great are You LORD! Father God, You are not only powerful, but You are power itself! You are strength and might! You make the seas boil and the mountains melt. Your power knows no bounds. Never let my mind wander from the fact that I serve the all-powerful creator God. You have made this universe, You own it, You will judge it, and You have power over every single thing within it. Never let my pitiful problems blind me from Your great power. How do I so quickly forget? I worry about my needs of things, yet my God has made all things! You are strong and mighty, nothing can stop You! God, You work all things to the good and You have even created all things with a purpose. You do not create carelessly. You have purposed all things to bring glory to Your name. Thank You Lord for remembering me. I love You Lord and I worship You and You alone. Great are You LORD and great is Your name king Jesus!

Psalm 114:8
Who turned the rock into a pool of water,
The flint into a fountain of waters.

Lord God, You are my Rock! There is no changing with You.
You forever remain the same and You can always be trusted to
be the same yesterday, today, and forevermore. And Lord, not
only are You forever the same, but You also feed me from that
same Rock. Lord, You have freely offered me Living Water.
Help me to seek that water daily. Help me to satisfy my thirst
by Your Son Jesus. This world offers many substitutes, but
only You truly satisfy. God, help me to thirst for You alone. Do
not let me fall prey to the lure of false cisterns that do not truly
satisfy. Every morning remind me that You are the only One
who satisfies. Let me seek the Rock and find my provision.
Help me to trust in You, even when it does not make worldly
sense. You are so, so good Lord. Thank You for saving me and
loving me. Bless Your mighty name.

Psalm 115:1
Not unto us, O Lord, not unto us, But to Your name give
glory, Because of Your mercy, Because of Your truth.

Lord, the day would end before I could list the reasons of why You
are worthy to be praised! But Lord, even for the sake of Your
mercy alone, my praises would never end. How can a God like
You, look down with loving eyes on a sinner like me? It is because
of Your great mercy. You are so loving and compassionate to us.
And even after saving us, You lead us in Your truth. You show us
Your ways and teach us how to live like the redeemed. Let us
always walk in Your truth, merciful God, and let us bring glory to
Your name. When we wander, I pray that You quickly correct us
and bring us home. I hate the feeling of falling way. Win back my
stubborn heart with Your love. Never let the things of this world
lure me away. I know that they all leave me empty, but You God,
You leave me filled. Guide me in Your truth Father and teach me to
walk in Your ways. Amen.

Psalm 115:11
You who fear the Lord, trust in the Lord;
He is their help and their shield.

Lord, I am ashamed to say that I do not always fear You as You have asked me to. I drift and wander and somehow I forget that You are right there by my side as I step into sin. I forget how it hurts You. I forget how much You truly detest all sin. That sin, great or small, has no place in Your presence and that You have called me to live in holiness, just as You are holy. That I was bought at a steep price and I should live in reflection of the great sacrifice that You gave. God, help me to always remember that You are watching. Help me to remember that You are always there, at my side, desiring for me to do good. God, I want to walk wisely. I want my life to bring You glory, not shame. Never let me get away with anything. Never let me think that I am alone. Convict me Lord, so that I never wander from Your path. Keep me in Your Word and let it guide me in truth. Help me to honor You all the days of my life.

Psalm 116:1-2
I love the Lord, because He has heard My voice and my
supplications. Because He has inclined His ear to me,
Therefore I will call upon Him as long as I live.

Oh LORD, how I love You! I am never alone! You are always there and You always hear my when I call. Thank You for being such a loving God. You hear Your children. You answer their calls. You always do what is best for us. I know that You hear and answer every prayer that I pray, even if I don't always understand how You have answered. Lord, Your ways are higher than my own and I cannot grasp what You have in store, but I know that it is good. You are good Lord and all that You do is good and just. I am still taken away with the fact that I have an audience with the King. That You hear me and my every need. Heaven forbid that I should ever feel alone because the God of the Universe is forever at my side. You hear me, and You lead me when I call. Oh Lord, how I love You! Thank You for Your amazing grace and thank You for the gift of Your Son.

Psalm 116:16-17

O Lord, truly I am Your servant; I am Your servant, the son of Your maidservant; You have loosed my bonds. I will offer to You the sacrifice of thanksgiving, And will call upon the name of the Lord.

Lord God, take me, I am Yours, I surrender. I want my life to be all for You. Can You please help me? Lord I am weak. Daily I struggle to give You all that You deserve, but I desire to. Lord Jesus, it is just as You said, the spirit is willing, but the flesh is so very weak. God, You have paid a price that I never could have paid. That alone was worth me giving my life for, but then You continue to bless me every day. God, every breath that You give me is a gift. So now let me offer that breath back to You in a song of praise. I pray that I exhale thanksgiving and praises to You. And when I am weak and when I stumble, I pray that I call upon Your name for strength. Lord, Father, King, please lead me. You lead and I will follow. Help me give my life up as a living sacrifice for all that You have done for me. If I could live one hundred times, I could never repay You for what You have done. Lord, I give You my life. Use me as You wish. Let me bring glory to Your name.

Psalm 116:8

For You have delivered my soul from death, My eyes from tears, And my feet from falling.

God, it continues to blow my mind that You have saved a sinner like me, but then You continue to bless me. Yes Lord, Your mercy is great. While I still sinned against You and lived my life according to my own will, You died for me. And now Lord, that I live for You, You continue to bless me. God, You have wiped the tears from my eyes and yet the tears of joy continue to abound. You are just so good to me. Lord, Your blessings are great and beyond compare. And Lord God, I thank You that You daily lead me down Your path. I pray that Your Word shines greatly in my life and shows me the way that You desire me to go. Be the lamp unto my feet and the light unto my path. Keep my feet from stumbling. Lord, keep me from evil, that Your name may be hallowed. I do not want to bring You shame. Help me to remain steadfast and close to Your promises.

Psalm 117:1-2

Praise the Lord, all you Gentiles! Laud Him, all you peoples! For His merciful kindness is great toward us, And the truth of the Lord endures forever. Praise the Lord!

Oh God, You are so good. I cannot wait for the day for when the whole world will praise Your name. When every man and every woman will lift their voices up together and sing praises to their King. You are so good to us and You are worthy to be praised. God, help me praise You every day. Do not let me only come to You in times of need. I want to always be praising You for the merciful kindness that You have shown towards me. And for the hope that You give me. How great is that hope! It is a blessed hope that helps me through every day. And Lord, for Your truth! While this world flows back and forth in its wishy-washy ways, You have given me a firm rock to stand upon. I want to stand upon Your Word all the days of my life. Your Word is truth. And so, I thank You Lord. Thank You for Your blessings, for Your great salvation, for Your merciful kindness, and for Your great truth that You have given me. Blessed be Your name.

146

Psalm 118:6
The Lord is on my side; I will not fear.
What can man do to me?

As Your Word says, "If God is for us, who can be against us?" God, You are on my side. Your go before me and You go behind me. You have paved the way to victory. Why do I still stumble? Why do I still fear? Strengthen me Lord, by the promises of Your Word. Help me to memorize those promises Lord that I may live by them. I have nothing to fear with You by my side. Let me trust in Your Word and find my strength in Your promises. Guide me, day by day, by Your Holy Spirit. You lead and I will follow. I am forever Yours Lord. Amen.

Psalm 118:8-9
It is better to trust in the Lord Than to put confidence in man. It is better to trust in the Lord Than to put confidence in princes.

LORD God, so often I will seek wisdom and advice from others long before I turn to You. Help me to quit this evil thing. Lord, let me turn to You first. God, if I am going to exhaust myself in trying to find help, I pray that I exhaust myself at Your feet alone. This world can neither save me nor even help me. You are my rock and Your are the anchor for my soul. Help me to rest upon You always. Help me to stay in Your Word and in prayer. Daily remind me of Your presence in my life. Man can never give me the peace that You alone can give. They cannot produce the joy within me like You do. You are God alone and Your ways are good and true. Help me to walk in those ways and forever trust in You.

Psalm 119:1-2

Blessed are the undefiled in the way, Who walk in the law of the Lord! Blessed are those who keep His testimonies, Who seek Him with the whole heart!

Lord Jesus, lead me in Your ways! Help me to follow You every day. Lord, I am like a fool who keeps going back and keeps doing the same things expecting different results. How often do I wander astray! You have shown me the way to go and yet I often find myself on my own. Help me to walk on the path that You have set before me. Help me to stay in Your Word so that it can guide me day by day. All that You say is good. Everything that You have taught me only leads to life. Do not let me be a fool Lord. Call me home when I have wandered and lead me by the sound of Your voice. My heart longs to follow You, but so often my flesh is weak. Give me the strength that I need to obey You. Help me to get out of my cycle of disobedience. I want to follow You and You alone.

Psalm 119:7

I will praise You with uprightness of heart, When I learn Your righteous judgments.

Oh Lord, how wonderful it is to praise You with a clean conscience. To come to You and ask You to search me and know me, and to find that I have been tested and found pure. It is only by the power of Your blood and Your Spirit that I can have this great peace. My only desire is to hear You say, "Well done." Keep me in Your ways Lord. Do not let me fall back into the life that You saved me from. Help me to forever be sensitive to what Your Spirit is speaking to me. Help me to love those around me as You did Jesus. You are my model. Let me daily seek Your guidance through Your Word and help me to live it out in everything that I do. Help me to walk in the Spirit.

Psalm 119:9
How can a young man cleanse his way?
By taking heed according to Your word.

Lord, I have tried so hard and so many ways to fix myself, yet I always will fall short. Yet, You promise to me that Your Word can cleanse me. Your Word can fix the error of my ways. Help me to be continually in Your Word. Let Your Word always be on my mind and on my lips. Father, I desire that You don't just save me, but that You save others through me. Put Your Word in my mouth that others may be comforted also. Use me as Your tool. Use me as Your messenger. Let me be an ambassador for Your Son Jesus and put a fire in my bones that bids me to call out "Be reconciled to God!" This world is lost Lord and only You can save it. Use me as You wish Lord, I am Yours.

Psalm 119:10-11
With my whole heart I have sought You; Oh, let me not
wander from Your commandments! Your word I have
hidden in my heart, that I might not sin against You!

Keep me Lord! Keep me in Your loving arms! LORD God, You have brought me so far. You have saved me from the pit I was trapped in and now I want to live my life for You and You alone. Help me to be the person that You want me to be. Never let me wander from Your side. I trust You Lord. Whatever it is that You need to do to and through me, I trust You. Whatever may come my way, I trust that You will work it to the good, as You have promised me, because I love You. Be forever on my heart and mind Father. I have no desire to sin against You. You are my God and my King! Help me to rest in Your lovingkindness. Help me to rest in Your Word.

Psalm 119:17
Deal bountifully with Your servant,
That I may live and keep Your word.

Lord God, let me never become wise in my own eyes. Even more so Father, never let me become wise in my own eyes concerning Your Word. Help me to come to Your Word daily with the wonder of a child. That I will always expect great things from every page that I read. You have given me all things that pertain to life and godliness. Where else can I turn? Only You have the Words of life! Yet often I become confident in my own plans. Heaven forbid that I become wise in my own eyes Father. Let me only seek the wisdom that You give. Let Your Word keep me from danger, let it keep me from folly, and let it keep me from sin. The power of Your Word is incomprehensible. So let me just read, and trust, that You are there, and You are working, and You hold this whole world in Your hands, by the power of Your Word.

Psalm 119:32
I will run the course of Your commandments,
For You shall enlarge my heart.

Oh Lord, how you have changed me! So often I can become disheartened by looking at the great distance I still have to go, but I should never forget about how far You have taken me. You have taken out my heart of stone and given me a heart of flesh. I once lived for myself, but now I live for my King and Savior, who loved me and died for me. Thank You Lord for the great work that You do. Thank You Lord for the grace that You have saved me by. You are an amazing God. There is no one like You. Lord, as Your servant wrote, eye has not seen, nor ear has heard, nor has entered into the heart of man the things which You have prepared for those who love You. Lord, this world does not know You, but we, Your children, we know You! You are amazing! Oh how I wish that You were my first morning thought and my last mediation of the day. Let me be consumed by You. And let my cup overflow into a dark and lost world that needs us, Your children, to be a light. Hallelujah Father. You are amazing!

Psalm 119:33-34

Teach me, O Lord, the way of Your statutes, And I shall keep it to the end. Give me understanding, and I shall keep Your law; Indeed, I shall observe it with my whole heart.

I am Yours. Lord God, it is as simple as that. I am Yours. Take of me what You will. Take all of me! I desire to hold nothing back from You. Lord God, if there is even a grain of sand that would separate me from You, I pray that You would remove it and cast it far away. I want You to have my all. Every part of me. Every ounce of my soul is Yours. Lord, teach me what I need to know so that I can be used by You. Help me to understand Your ways so that I can follow them to the fullest. Break my heart for what breaks Yours. Keep me from sin Father! Keep me from sin. Revive me and make me whole again. All I want to do is serve You. Do not let me stumble when I am weak. Protect me from the evil one and his servants. LORD, be my God!

Psalm 119:37

Turn away my eyes from looking at worthless things, And revive me in Your way.

Lord Jesus, You have bought me. You purchased me at a great price. Your grace may be free, but it is certainly not cheap. Help me to give my all to You. And Lord, save me from my weakness. There are so many things in this world that entice me, but they all are going to burn. As You have said, I must set my eyes on the things of heaven. I must store up heavenly riches where moth and rust do not destroy. Lord, turn my eyes from looking at worthless things! Set my eyes on Your kingdom! Do not let me be lured away by the cares and riches of this world. Grow me in Your Spirit and Your Word that I might bear fruit! Give me the strength to cast away my idols. You are my God and You alone! I love You Lord and You know that. Thank You for being my strength when I am weak. Now Lord, please be the treasure that I seek.

151

Psalm 119:41-42

Let Your mercies come also to me, O Lord-- Your salvation according to Your word. So shall I have an answer for him who reproaches me, For I trust in Your word.

Oh Lord, let me find great peace in Your promises and Your Truth. I want to rest in Your tender mercies. You have given me peace through Your Son. God, give me words to speak when those who don't know You attack. Let me know when to keep my words few and when to boldly stand up against them. Father, I desire to represent You to the fullest. Let my words be full of grace and truth. Help me to speak out against sin with passion, zeal, and tears in my eyes. Let those whom I witness to know that I have a godly fear for their lives and that I love them as You have commanded me to. Help me to be as gentle as a dove and yet as cunning as a serpent. Let me be more like Your Son Jesus. Amen.

Psalm 119:48

My hands also I will lift up to Your commandments, Which I love, And I will meditate on Your statutes.

I will love the LORD my God with all of my heart, mind, soul and strength. I will trust You and I will obey You. I ask You to search my heart, know me, test me and try me, and if You find anything within me that You do not desire, tell me. Tell me Lord and I will forsake it. And as I seek You with my whole heart, I will rest in Your great peace. A peace that surpasses understanding that no other person or thing can give me. God, You give me liberty! I no longer have to walk in fear. I know that You have done a great work in me and I know that You will continue to finish that work as You have promised. You are so good to me Lord. Thank You for Your amazing grace. Let me boldly proclaim, You are my King! Hallelujah!

Psalm 119:50
This is my comfort in my affliction,
For Your word has given me life.

Lord, where was I before You found me? Before You called
me to You? I do not know how I got by, but now Your
Word leads me and guides me, day by day. Help me to
never forget Your promises. Your Word has an answer for
every trial I will face. When trials, persecution, and
temptation come my way, I can take shelter in Your Word.
In it, I find all that I need for this life. Direction for every
challenge I face and answers to my questions. Help me to
daily be near Your Word. For it has given me life. Hide
Your Word in my heart Father. Bring it to my mind when
my troubles seem great. And remind me that You hold the
whole world in Your hands and that You spoke it into
existence. Nothing is too great for You. You are the Alpha
and the Omega, the beginning and end, the Creator God,
and You have made all things through Your Word. Thank
You Lord for who You are.

Psalm 119:61
The cords of the wicked have bound me, But I have not
forgotten Your law.

Lord, in these last days the wicked try to pervert Your
Word, but I will never forsake it. They call good things evil
and evil things good. They call Your Word irrelevant or out
dated, but I will never turn from the Words of truth! Only
You have the words that give life Father. While some may
veer to the right or to the left, I will continue down the paths
that You have set me on. I will trust in the well walked
paths of those who have gone before me. Your Word is
truth! Oh how I wish You would open their eyes and let
them see the glory of Your Word. The beauty and majesty
of Your holy Word. It gives me peace and assurance. It
guides me in all that I need to do. Help me to forever cling
to Your Word and to Your son Jesus.

Psalm 119:63
I am a companion of all who fear You,
And of those who keep Your precepts.

Thank You Lord for making me a part of Your great family.
To adopt me as Your child and to make me an heir in Your
kingdom. And You have put me among so many other
children of God. I am immediately at home with those who
seek Your face and love Your ways. There is a great bond that
we share through Your Son Jesus. Though I may have just met
them, our bond is deep because of Your Holy Spirit working in
us. Help me to walk in this brotherly love, as You have
commanded me to. Though I can pick my friends, I cannot
pick my family which you have brought me into. Help me to
love all of my brothers and sisters. Help me to weep with those
who weep and rejoice with those who rejoice. Remind me to
confess my trespasses so that we can pray for one another. And
let the world see the godly love that we have for one another.

Psalm 119:64
The earth, O Lord, is full of Your mercy;
Teach me Your statutes.

LORD God, forgive me if I am ever ungrateful for all that You
do for me. Forgive me if I ever doubt Your lovingkindness.
Forgive me for when I do not trust in Your promises. For this
whole world is full of Your mercies! I see them every day, but
I do not acknowledge them. Lord, You are the air that I
breathe. Father, I do not even realize where I would be without
You. How many times have you saved me without my
knowing? How much pain have You prevented without my
knowledge? And Lord, how many times have You allowed me
to suffer, because You knew that I needed it? God You are
good and Your ways are true. Help me to only ever trust in
Your promise that You will work all things to the good for
those who love You and are called according to Your
purposes. God, the whole earth is filled with Your mercies.
Help me to see them. Amen.

Psalm 119:67 & 71

Before I was afflicted I went astray, But now I keep Your word. It is good for me that I have been afflicted, That I may learn Your statutes.

Lord, no punishment is pleasant in the moment, but I know that it is for a reason. Help me to see when You are chastising me. Help me to sense when You are trying to teach me a lesson. I do not even know how many times I stray in a day. More than I would think. Yet You lovingly woo me back. Lord, You could strong arm me back into Your presence, but You choose to just afflict me with what I can bear so that I come back to You. You love me so much, You won't leave me as I am. You refine me and perfect me. You keep on sanctifying me beyond what I ever imagined. God, if I veer off course, correct me quickly. You know how I can be! Correct me quickly so that I do not go far from You. If I am stubborn, use whatever force is necessary to bring me to my senses. How else would I learn? Keep me in Your ways Father. Help me to give You my all.

Psalm 119:73

Your hands have made me and fashioned me; Give me understanding, that I may learn Your commandments.

Lord, I am who You made me to be. Before I was conceived You had a plan for me. Everything about me is just the way You knew it would be. You crafted me for a purpose. Help me to know what it is You desire from me. Help me to see what my calling is and how I am supposed to use my gifts to better serve Your kingdom. Lord, Your Word tells me that You have a plan, please now give me understanding so that I can give You my best. I want to serve You with my whole heart. You and You alone. Teach me Your ways so that I can follow them. Show me my calling so that I can serve with all my heart. And remind me that I am Yours and that You made me for a purpose. Thank You Lord.

Psalm 119:88
Revive me according to Your lovingkindness,
So that I may keep the testimony of Your mouth.

Blessed be my great God and King. Hallowed be Your name. Lord, I want to bring You glory and praise in all that I do. I desire for all those who see me to know that I serve a great and powerful God. For Your great name's sake, revive me Lord. Revive me so that I can serve You zealously. Revive me so that I can walk in Your truth. Lord God, be the fuel in my fire. Strengthen me and uplift me, for no other reason than to bring You praise. I pray that my life would be a sweet song to You. That all I do would be seasoned with grace and a reflection of Your Son. Jesus, be my vision. Be my hope and be my guide. Help me to follow Your example. Help me to bring glory to my King.

Psalm 119:94
I am Yours, save me; For I have sought Your precepts.

Lord God, I am Yours! My heart is Yours, my life is Yours, all that I have I want to give to You. Save me Lord! And keep on saving me! Hold me close to You and draw me ever close each day. Complete the good work that You have begun in me, as You have promised. Mold me into the tool that You desire to use and have me always be near Your side so that I am ready. Lord, though my actions may fail, You alone know the desire of my heart. I am Yours Lord. Be my strength when I am weak. Save me from my sin. Keep me from temptations and guide me down Your path. I want to give You my all. I love You Lord. You are so, so good.

Psalm 119:103
How sweet are Your words to my taste,
Sweeter than honey to my mouth!

Lord Jesus, You were tempted in all ways and yet You did not sin. You know what I have gone through and You know what I am going to face. Protect me from the evil one and his demons. This world tries to lure me away with every temptation imaginable, yet when I hear Your still calm voice, You call me home. I return to Your Word and it is so good. Why do I ever become distracted by entertainment and folly when You Word is so very satisfying? Like water in a dry land, Your Word refreshes me when I am weak. When I am scared or confused, Your Word puts me back on Your path. When the enemy tries to trick me with his lies, Your Word reminds me that You are faithful, loving, and true. Thank You for Your Word Lord. Help me to learn it and help me to live it. Let Your Word always be on my lips.

Psalm 119:112
I have inclined my heart to perform Your statutes Forever,
to the very end.

Lord God, You know me. You know how much I love You. You know greatly I desire to serve You. Help me to live out the faith that I desire to live. God, in my heart I have determined to be faithful, but my heart can be so fickle at times. And while my spirit is even more than willing, my flesh can be so incredibly weak. Save me Lord. Strengthen me. By the power of Your Holy Spirit, keep me, until the very end. Help my heart become more like Your heart and strengthen me so that I may keep Your ways. And if I fall or if I fail, help me to get back up again quickly and continue down Your path. Send help, restore me, and move me on. Do not let me wallow in my failures. Remind me of Your amazing and unending grace and lead me in the way everlasting. I love You Lord, amen.

Psalm 119:116-117

Uphold me according to Your word, that I may live; And do not let me be ashamed of my hope. Hold me up, and I shall be safe, And I shall observe Your statutes continually.

Lord, I do not need much. Just lead me and keep me. That is all I ask. Lead me in Your ways, do not let me wander or stray. Do not let me be fooled by the doctrines of men, but help me to discern Your truth. And keep me from temptation, keep me from sin, and keep me from shaming Your holy name. I know that You can do all these things. You are God. You are the I AM. You are my Savior and my King. If You promise to keep me, I trust that You are able. Comfort me with the words of Your mouth and let me rest in Your great love. Be my king and I will follow Your ways all of my life. Let me feel Your presence each day as I seek You. Yes, let me feel Your loving arms around me. There is no greater feeling than Your amazing love.
Hallelujah Father.

Psalm 119:124-125

Deal with Your servant according to Your mercy, And teach me Your statutes. I am Your servant; Give me understanding, That I may know Your testimonies.

Lord God, I am Your servant. You lead and I will follow. You command and I will obey. Lord, if I ever stumble or fall, deal with me according to Your lovingkindness. You know what I need and what will serve me best. I know that in my weakness I would ask You for smooth sailing in this life, but that is not what I truly want. I want to serve You and if that means I will be a bumpy road at times, so be it Lord. Guide me, lead me, push me, and pull me. Make me into a tool fit for the Master's use. Make me into soldier who can wield the Sword of the Lord, the Word of God. Let me not just exist, but be a fighter for You my King. Give me understanding. Teach me Your ways. And lead me in the way everlasting.

Psalm 119:132

Look upon me and be merciful to me, As Your custom is toward those who love Your name.

O God, how I love Your ways! You are so good to Your children. You give us more than we could ever deserve. Those who love You, You love so much more abundantly. And we love You because You first loved us. God, guide my steps each day and keep me on Your path. Lord, do not let sin reign in me. Give me the strength to cast it far from me. Help me to crucify my flesh and stay in prayer, lest I fall into temptation. Show those around me that You care for Your children and that You always provide for those who love You. Shine through Your people Lord. Shine bright.

Psalm 119:136

Rivers of water run down from my eyes, Because men do not keep Your law.

Lord, help me to hate sin and to mourn over the lost. It is so easy for me to become complacent with my life. Give me Your heart and help me to weep for those who are lost and perishing. Help me to not remain silent concerning sin. Give me the strength to speak out against those who do evil and let me mourn over them. Let rivers of water flow from my eyes. Help me to reach out to them and let them see the pain that I grieve over them. Do not let me come across as self-righteous or as one who has arrived. Break my heart for these people Lord. You do not rejoice over the death of the wicked. You desire to see all men be saved. Give me Your heart Father. Let me be Your hands and feet.

Psalm 119:147-148

I rise before the dawning of the morning, And cry for help; I hope in Your word. My eyes are awake through the night watches, That I may meditate on Your word.

Father God, let me be more like Your servant David. Teach me to rise before the dawn to seek Your face. Teach me to meditate on Your ways before I lay myself down to sleep. Do not let me become distracted by the things of this life. Do not let me look to any other thing for refuge. My hope is in You and You alone. My mind wanders and thinks of silly things, useless things, or wicked things. Help me to keep my mind clean and focused on You. Your Word leads me and guides me. Let me be in Your Word continually. Let me find You there in the morning and night hours. Reveal Yourself to me through Your holy Word.

Psalm 119:160

The entirety of Your word is truth, And every one of Your righteous judgments endures forever.

Father, help me to trust in You always. Help me to trust in Your Word. Remove any doubt that I may struggle with and let me find peace in knowing that Your Word is truth. There is not a single fault in Your Word. It is perfect. And it will never change because You never change God. Thank You for being so steadfast and unchanging. I never have to wonder about Your faithfulness because Your promises endure forever. You don't get moody and leave me. You don't have bad days. You are the unchanging and unchangeable Creator God. You are my rock and my firm foundation. Thank You for the peace that I can find when I trust in You.

Psalm 119:163
I hate and abhor lying, But I love Your law.

Lord, teach me to hate sin like Your servant David did. This world tries to convince me of accepting sin, but I know that You hate sin. Sin cannot be in Your presence. And it is my sins that separate me from You. Lord, there are no small sins. There is no insignificant sin. You will judge all sin whether in condemnation or on the cross. Lord, You bought me at a price. Remind me that Your grace was given freely, but it was not cheap! It cost You Your Son. So Father, help me to hate lying, to hate cheating, pride, and greed. Help me to walk uprightly and do not let sin cling to me.

Psalm 119:165
Great peace have those who love Your law, And nothing causes them to stumble.

My strength may fail, my plans may fall apart, my eyes may grow weary, but I will not stumble God, for Your Word stands strong forever. Oh, help me to trust in Your Word dear Father. Help me to have its passages flowing through my mind all day long. Let every obstacle I face be met with one of Your promises. Let every disappointment be met by Your everlasting declarations of love towards me. Your Word has an answer to every problem and a solution to every situation I face. Immerse me in Your Word and let its truth flow into every part of me life. Let the peace that surpasses understanding come upon me as I continue to grow in the fullness of Your Truth, Your Word, and Your Son. Thank You Abba Father for Your everlasting goodness and Your Word. May it ever be on my lips.

Psalm 119:176

I have gone astray like a lost sheep; Seek Your servant, For I do not forget Your commandments.

God, sometimes I wander and stray. Things in my life creep in and soon I find myself far from You. I get lost and I begin to feel the effects of being distant. Seek Your sheep. When I wander, bring me back. And when I stray, be quick to correct. I never forget Your commandments. I never forget Your Word. They just become drowned out by a busy world and a busy life. Come and find me when I stray. Like a sheep, I often get lost and I only know my way back when I hear the voice of my Shepherd. I love You Lord because You first loved me. Keep me by Your side. Amen.

Psalm 120:1

In my distress I cried to the Lord, And He heard me.

O Lord, the enemy may try to make me think that You do not hear me, but I know that You do. You hear my cries. You hear my thoughts. And You even hear those things inside of me that I wish You did not hear. You are always with me and I know that You answer my prayers. I do not always understand how You are working in my life, but I trust that You are working. Deliver me God, from my troubles and my fears. And most of all, deliver me from my own foolish self. So often I am my own worst enemy, but I know that You are working. I know that You are working inside of me. Heal me by Your Spirit Lord. Purify me and make me useful for Your service. Help me be more like Jesus! Amen.

Psalm 121:1-2

I will lift up my eyes to the hills-- From whence comes my help?
My help comes from the Lord, Who made heaven and earth.

Father, help me to keep my eyes on You! You are my
strength. You are the source of my peace. And You are the
Almighty God. You made the heavens and the earth. You
made the trees and the stars. How small can my problems be
for You? Lord, what looks like mountains to me is less than
dust for You. Help me to trust that if I call on You, You will
answer. Remind me, Lord, that nothing is outside of Your
hands. And Lord, You do not sleep! You are always
watching and always waiting. Whenever I look towards
You, You are ready to go another round. Thank You for
always being there for me Lord. I love You.

Psalm 122:1

I was glad when they said to me,
"Let us go into the house of the Lord."

Oh how wonderful it is to gather together with my brethren.
There's no place I'd rather be Lord, than with my brothers
and my sisters. Father, help my heart to never be deceived.
God, I ask that You protect my church from the enemy, the
father of lies, the divider, the deceiver. Do not let him bring
division amongst Your people. I pray for my own heart and
the heart of my brethren that we would rejoice in the
privilege of gathering together. Help Your people to long
for fellowship. Remind me of how important fellowship is.
Let me be glad for every opportunity that I have to gather.
Let me never forsake it! Oh God, too many have begun to
forsake our gathering together! Bring them home Father.
Let Your family rejoice in our gathering together to worship
You. I pray that all we do is holy and acceptable in Your
sight. Bless our efforts Lord and bless our fellowship.

Psalm 122:6 & 9
Pray for the peace of Jerusalem: "May they prosper who love you." Because of the house of the Lord our God I will seek your good.

Lord God, as You have asked of me in Your Word, I pray, "bring peace to Jerusalem." At the center of Your creation is Your holy city. I pray that You would touch the heart of Your people and bring them back to You. Show them Jesus Father. Bring to them their Messiah and have Him rule in their hearts. Protect Your city from its enemies. Do not let them prevail. The whole world rallies against Your people, yet You have preserved them through the greatest of trials. Even in their unfaithfulness, You remain faithful. And that brings me peace Father, because if You remain faithful to them, I know that You will remain faithful to me.

Psalm 123:1
Unto You I lift up my eyes, O You who dwell in the heavens.

Father God, when this world gets crazy and I don't know what to do, help me to lift my eyes up to You. Lord, when I am faced with temptation, or anger, or despair, help me to lift my eyes up to You. God, each day as I am faced with numerous decisions to make, decisions to obey or to disobey, decisions to face the enemy or to take the easy road, Lord, help me to lift my eyes up to You. I know where my help comes from. Your Spirit leads me and guides me. Help me to be looking. Help me to be listening. Father, help me to always be lifting my eyes up to You. I know how failure comes. It comes when I look to myself. It comes when I hold my struggles close. It comes when I get my eyes off of You. Oh Lord, help me to keep my eyes forever fixed upon You, until Your mercy comes.
Thank You Lord, amen.

Psalm 123:3-4

Have mercy on us, O Lord, have mercy on us! For we are exceedingly filled with contempt. Our soul is exceedingly filled With the scorn of those who are at ease, With the contempt of the proud.

Lord God, transform my heart. My flesh continually becomes worked up when I don't understand why things happen. I see the wicked prosper and the righteous suffer. I see men and women in sin and they mock You. I understand David when he says, "How long Lord will You allow the wicked to prosper?" But Father, You are just so longsuffering. And I quickly forget that just as You are patient with them, You are also patient with me also. Thank You for being so gracious Lord. Help me remember how often You show me grace and remind me to keep praying for those who have not yet received it. Have mercy on me Lord. Oh, how I need You. Amen Lord, Amen.

Psalm 124:1

If it had not been the Lord who was on our side,

"If it had not been the LORD who was on our side…" Wow, Lord. Where can I go from here? Where would I be today if You had not saved me? Where would I be if Your Spirit had not been working inside of me? How many tragedies have You saved me from that I don't even know about? How many blessings have I received, not knowing that they were directly from You? Someday I will know Lord, but until that day, when we see You face to face, I will just trust in You. God, You are my help and my strong tower where I come for shelter. I do not know where I would be without You Lord, but I pray that You keep me by Your side, for now, and forever more. Amen.

Psalm 124:2
"If it had not been the Lord who was on our side,

Oh my Lord, where would I be without You? What path would I have been wandering on if You had not found me? What sorrow would I have beheld? God, You picked me up out of the mire and You have placed me on solid ground. You have given me a sure foundation and You have gifted me with the tools and the supplies in which to build with. All that I have is from You Father. Every good and perfect thing has been given to me according to Your grace. LORD God, I am thankful for how kindly You have dealt with me. I am humbled by Your mercies. While I would have wandered and strayed, You called me home. You have brought me back Lord, and now I desire to serve You and You alone. Thank You for saving me Father. Your mercies are never ending. Amen.

Psalm 124:6
Blessed be the Lord,
Who has not given us as prey to their teeth.

Lord God, I thank You for all the things You have done for me which I am totally clueless about. So often I am quick to become frustrated because everything does not turn out the way I desired, but I realize that I have no clue as to what You have saved me from. You have protected me from countless disasters, injuries, and failures which I will never know about this side of eternity. You did not let me stumble. You did not forsake me. And best of all, here I am today, still seeking Your face. God, You could have given up on me, but You didn't. In fact, You have promised me that You never will. God, Your mercy blows my mind. Your longsuffering humbles me. Your grace, it overwhelms me. You are so good to me Lord. Bless Your holy name. You are good!

Psalm 125:1-2

Those who trust in the Lord Are like Mount Zion, Which cannot be moved, but abides forever. As the mountains surround Jerusalem, So the Lord surrounds His people From this time forth and forever.

God, if You are for us, truly, who can be against us? I hold my troubles close to me and the closer I hold them, the larger they appear. Help me to push them far away from me and focus on the power of my God and King. You protect me and You are for me. You have plans for me, plans of good and not evil. When I put my trust in You, nothing on this earth can shake me. Those who don't know You cannot understand the peace that You give. Lord, Your presence surrounds me and you dwell within me. You go before me and You take up the rear. Help me to trust and to rest in Your saving power. Help me to trust in Your Spirit. Lead me God, now, and forever more.

Psalm 125:4

Do good, O Lord, to those who are good, And to those who are upright in their hearts.

Father, though I know You are good and You bless us all more than we deserve, I would never want to miss out on a blessing simply because I did not ask. So here I am Lord. I humbly ask You, "bless Your servants." God, for myself, my family, my church, and for all the believers I know, those who are worshiping You in spirit and truth, bless them. Lord God, bless the pastors that have not compromised Your Holy Word. Bless the evangelist who painstakingly is rejected time and time again, but still carries on. Bless the new believer who desires to grow and whom Satan desires to discourage. Bless the servants who hold Your Church together. Bless the teachers who hide Your Word in our children's' hearts. Bless the prayer warriors, who fight behind the scenes and win more battles for us than we'll ever know. "Do good, O LORD, to those who are good." Bless us Lord and do it all for Thy Name's sake.

167

Psalm 126:3
The Lord has done great things for us, And we are glad.

Oh Lord, You make me glad. You bring me joy. You fill me up when I am empty and dry. You have done so much for me. Too often I forget of Your goodness. Too often I do not count my blessings. But God, You have done great things for us. Lord, when I was foolish and in sin, You prepared a way for me. When I still rejected You, You loved me. Before I ever called out to You, You were listening for me. God You saved me. You have forgiven me, adopted me, and given me a purpose and a calling. Lord, I am grateful and glad that You are my God. Help me to never forget all that You have done for me. Help me to always pray with thanksgiving. Help me to count my blessings each day Lord. I am blessed far better than I deserve. Thank You God and praise Your Holy Name.

Psalm 126:5-6
Those who sow in tears Shall reap in joy. He who continually goes forth weeping, Bearing seed for sowing, Shall doubtless come again with rejoicing, Bringing his sheaves with him.

Lord Jesus, help me to sow tears like You did. I want to weep over Jerusalem and her rejection of You. I want to weep over those who are perishing. Lord, I want to sow my tears in weeping, and I want to reap the joy that comes through my answered prayers. Lord, do not let my prayers be void of emotion. Do not let them lack devotion. Help me to pray with power and passion. Help me to pray without doubt or ceasing. Help me to be as passionate about prayer as I am about life itself. You have promised Your children so many things, yet we often fail to pray to receive them. Help Your people to pray Lord. Help us to pray with tears.

Psalm 127:1-2

Unless the Lord builds the house, They labor in vain who build it; Unless the Lord guards the city, The watchman stays awake in vain. It is vain for you to rise up early, To sit up late, To eat the bread of sorrows; For so He gives His beloved sleep.

Father, sometimes I try too hard, when all You want me to do is give up. I work so hard, yet You want me to stop. Help me to not trust in my own strength. Help me to look to You for my strength. I can try so hard and work so hard, but if I am not doing it by Your power, it will be for nothing. If I must strive to gain, I will have to strive to maintain, but if You build the house, You will sustain it by Your power. Let me work hard, not trusting in my own labors, but in Your faithfulness to bless my work. Give me ears to hear You guide me. Help me not try to force things that are not Your will. Give me a heart like Your Son Jesus. Not my will be done Father, but Your will be done. Amen.

Psalm 127:3-5

Behold, children are a heritage from the Lord, The fruit of the womb is a reward. Like arrows in the hand of a warrior, So are the children of one's youth. Happy is the man who has his quiver full of them; They shall not be ashamed, But shall speak with their enemies in the gate.

Lord God, thank You for my family. You have given them to me and You have put them into my life for a reason. Help me to pray for them. Help me to serve them. Help me to fulfill the role that You have given to me concerning them. You spoke wisely to mothers and fathers and to children and siblings. You have directed me in how I am to live and how our family can bring You glory. I pray that we all can serve You with all that we have. Be with my family this day Lord. Watch over them and draw them ever closer to You. I pray that You grow my family in both size and godliness. That we would be a group of people who are known for bringing glory to God. Use us Father. And please use me to help lift them up.

Psalm 128:1-3

Blessed is every one who fears the Lord, Who walks in His ways. When you eat the labor of your hands, You shall be happy, and it shall be well with you. Your wife shall be like a fruitful vine. In the very heart of your house, Your children like olive plants All around your table.

Father, help me to be content with all that You have given me. Satan would tempt me to desire things that satisfy my flesh, but You are wise and have better plans for me. Help me to lead a simple and pure life. Let my heart long for nothing more than Your will for me and for the family You have given me. Help me to fear You Lord, with a godly fear. Help me to walk in Your ways. Lord, let me work hard and be satisfied with the fruit of my labors. Bless my family Lord. Let all of us seek Your face and honor You in all that we do. Help me to lead my house to serve the Lord. Let my table be surrounded by cheerfulness and thanksgiving. Let our beds be covered in prayer. Every morning let us seek You. Every night let us thank You. Help my family be one that honors the LORD. You are good.

Psalm 128:4

Behold, thus shall the man be blessed Who fears the Lord.

Lord God, I want You to bless me abundantly. Firstly, I want You to bless me by using me. I want to be Your tool. Use me to save lost souls, to build up Your Church, and to bring glory to Your name. Next Lord, bless me by making me holy. Help me to live a life that is holy and pure. Save me from my own evil self and lead me in Your righteous paths. Sanctify me and make me more like Your Son Jesus each day. Teach me to reverence You and adore You. Teach me to bring You honor, glory, and praise. And lastly Lord, as You see fit and beneficial, bless my life here on this earth. I know that You will always provide for my needs and all that is above that is just more of Your amazing grace. Bless me Lord and teach me to fear You.

Psalm 129:2

Many a time they have afflicted me from my youth; Yet they have not prevailed against me.

Lord, day by day I never quite know what to expect, but I know that in the end, You win. You have promised us victory. Victory in eternal life and victory over sin. People may hurt me, things may break, but You will carry us through until the end. As long as I continue to draw close to You, this world cannot prevail against me. I will always find victory through Jesus Christ my Lord. Again Lord, if You are for us, who can be against us? Help me to remember that when things look bad. Help me to remember these promises when all looks hopeless. Remind me that there will always be hope if my hope is in You.

Psalm 129:3

The plowers plowed on my back They made their furrows long.

O Lord my God, be the God of my house! Be the God of my children! Be the God of my parents! Be the God of my siblings and my spouse! Oh Lord, how I long to be a household that seeks Your face. That generations would spring forth and all live to serve You. Help me teach Your ways to the youth. Help me model Your ways for the old. God, use me in my family. Father, I beg of You, save them and keep them close to Your side. Pour out Your Spirit upon my home. Let Your praises be shared around my table. Let all we do be to bless and serve You. Help us to pray, Lord. Help us to be in Your Word. Help us to surrender our lives to You. Help my house to serve the LORD.

Psalm 129:4
The Lord is righteous;
He has cut in pieces the cords of the wicked.

Lord, whether it be the people from my past, or even just the old me, they would try to drag me back. My flesh fights against me and tries to pin me down. This whole world is against my progress towards You, but God, You break every chain and You loose every cord. You can help me strip off every weight that burdens my walk. I have tried to fight and strive to be free, but You alone are able to free me from the wicked. You alone can set me free. I desire to be free Lord. Free from sin and free from the old me. LORD God almighty, make me new and set me free. Free to live for You. I give You all that I have and all that I am. Make me Yours, forever. Amen.

Psalm 130:1-2
Out of the depths I have cried to You, O Lord; Lord, hear
my voice! Let Your ears be attentive To the voice of my
supplications.

Here I am God! You see me! You know me! You know my wanderings and my struggles. You know my every thought. Father, hear my voice and come to my aid. I am dependent on You Lord. Without You I am nothing. Without You I am but dust. Hear the cry of my prayers. Let me know that you are listening. Show Yourself again in my life. Lord, I cry out from the depths, but You are with me. You have always remained faithful and true, but I often wander. Do not remain silent oh Lord. Hear my prayers. Answer my petitions. Show Yourself strong on behalf of Your children. I have nothing to bring You. Nothing to offer You. I appeal to Your great mercy and kindness. Your goodness and longsuffering is all I can hope in. Lord, You have heard my prayer and now I await Your answer. Speak, for Your servant listens.

Psalm 130:3
If You, Lord, should mark iniquities,
O Lord, who could stand?

If You, LORD, should mark iniquities, O Lord, who could stand? O God, my God, if You were not so gracious, where would I be? O Lord Most High, if I were judge, how many times would I have condemned myself? Your mercies are never ending. Your promises are never failing. Your love is ever abounding. O LORD God, who is like You? Grace upon grace and mercies upon mercies. You pour out Your love upon Your children. Father, I can hardly imagine what my fate would be if You gave me what I deserved. Yet You don't. You pour out amazing mercies upon me and You love me in spite of me. Thank You Lord for Your great kindness. Thank You for Your Son. Thank You for the cross.

Psalm 130:5-6
I wait for the Lord, my soul waits, And in His word I do hope. My soul waits for the Lord More than those who watch for the morning-- Yes, more than those who watch for the morning

Lord God, You have promised me so many great things in Your Word. All that I could ever need from life You have addressed. You have given me an answer for all that I seek. Now please help me to wait on Your promises. I trust that You will be faithful, as You always have, but I must patiently wait for all things to come to pass. Oh Lord, how I long for you to complete the work that You have begun in me. Jesus, I long for Your coming. How much longer must we wait? Yet I will wait. I will patiently wait for You. You are God and You are good and I know that all things are working together for Your good plan in my life. Please just help me remain obedient as I wait for You. Give me the strength to keep on serving.

Psalm 131:1

Lord, my heart is not haughty, Nor my eyes lofty. Neither do I concern myself with great matters, Nor with things too profound for me.

Here I am God. Once again I come before You in prayer, but today I just want to come in simplicity. Here I am. Take me and use me. I trust that You are currently meeting my every need, so I just desire to remain open to what You want from me. How may I serve You this day Lord? How may I be of use to my King? I give You my life. I give You my soul. Take all of me Lord. Whatever it is You may desire, I freely give. Help me to hear You. Help me to listen. Keep me sensitive to Your Spirit this day. Prick my heart and point me where You would want me to go. I am wholly Yours Father. Use me as You desire and fill me with Your Spirit. Amen.

Psalm 132:3-5

Surely I will not go into the chamber of my house, Or go up to the comfort of my bed; I will not give sleep to my eyes Or slumber to my eyelids, Until I find a place for the Lord, A dwelling place for the Mighty One of Jacob.

Oh God, I wish that I could live for You as David did. That Your glory would be the focus of my days. That I would have a heart that would give anything to be with You. Father, help me never to settle for less than Your best. Rouse me when I am weary! Correct me when I stray! Help me to be the child whom loves You wholeheartedly! Oh, that I would give You all of my days. Oh, that I would live a life that was pleasing in Your eyes. My whole life I desire to lay before You Lord. Crucify my flesh and let no evil thing remain within me. Stir my soul each morning, that I might seek Your face! Oh, that I might know the heights, and depths, and breadth of Your great love for me. Take my life God, I give it freely. I am Yours Father.
I am Yours. Hallelujah!

Psalm 132:7
Let us go into His tabernacle;
Let us worship at His footstool.

Oh my God, here I am to worship You! You are amazing and beyond the words of any poet. Your beauty surpasses the skill of any artist. Your comfort exceeds any song. Your goodness is immeasurable. Your holiness is untouchable. Lord, Your will is unstoppable. You alone have all power, and might, and strength, and splendor. You are my God and I worship You. Lord, humbly I bow before You. Let this saying never become old or petty, You are the maker of heaven and earth. LORD God, You spoke the universe into existence. You hold all things together with Your mighty hand and one day You will let it all go. All these things we know will burn away with fervent heat. All things will pass away except for Your Holy Word. You will make a new heavens and a new earth. All of this marvelous splendor, and yet You have invited me to sit at Your table. You blow me away Lord. Words cannot express Your awesomeness. Praise Your holy and mighty name.

Psalm 133:1
Behold, how good and how pleasant it is For brethren to dwell together in unity!

Lord God, I pray that You give me a Spirit of unity. Help me to crucify my own flesh, be rid of my own desires, and selflessly serve my brothers and sisters. Jesus, be my model and my guide. Teach me to live like You did. Help me to serve those in need and to esteem others more highly than I do myself. Lord, I can be so selfish at times. Let me become selfless! Help me to bring unity where there is division. Help me to speak uplifting words this day. Do not let me speak anything that would tear down, but only speak words which lift up. I pray that my conduct would show others Your love and that my actions would point people to You. I am not good Father, but I have You working in me. Let this be my testimony. It isn't me, but Him who is working in me.

176

Psalm 134:1-2

Behold, bless the Lord, All you servants of the Lord, Who by night stand in the house of the Lord! Lift up your hands in the sanctuary, And bless the Lord.

God, it is so hard sometimes to look beyond the pains and struggles of each day and focus on Your beauty. I can become disconnected and lose my desire to praise You. But God, You command me to praise You. Even when I do not feel like it, I should lift up my hands to You and remember the great things You have done. You have done amazing things in my life, You have given me more than I deserve, and yet the smallest of problems makes me hesitant to praise You. Help me to have a heart of praise Father. Help me to lift my hands and praise You. I desire to come before You and worship You this day. Turn my heart into a heart of joy because of Your lovingkindness. You are good Lord, and I praise You for it.

Psalm 135:5-6

For I know that the Lord is great, And our Lord is above all gods. Whatever the Lord pleases He does, In heaven and in earth, In the seas and in all deep places.

LORD God, Your ways are higher than my ways and they go far beyond my own understanding. Why have You placed me where I am? Why have You set this path before me? What is Your purpose in my afflictions? When will I find Your peace and rest? I do not know, but I know that You are good. You do as You please and You do only what is best in Your eyes. God, help me to trust in Your goodness and Your plans. I may not know Your reasons, but I know You. You love me, You care for me, and You have a plan for me. Help me to be listening for Your directions. Help me to follow You when You call. God, bear with me in my weaknesses. Let my life bring You glory Father.
Forever and ever.

Psalm 135:10-11

He defeated many nations And slew mighty kings-- Sihon king of the Amorites, Og king of Bashan, And all the kingdoms of Canaan

Oh Lord God Almighty, You have defeated many great foes. By Your power, You have slain Og of Bashan and many other giants that stood before Your people. I pray that You would be my God Who fights my giants. I pray that I have no fear as I stand before them. That I would go in and possess the promises that You have set before me. Let me fear no giant. Let me fear no evil. My God and My King fights for me! He protects me and He guides me. You, Oh God, go before me and You prepare a path. You Lord, go behind me and protect my flanks. Your goodness encompasses me Father. Lord, help me to go. Help me to go up and take those promises which I have left untouched far too long. Lead me into the battle Lord, for I know that the enemy is in Your hands. Help me to fight for You Lord and give You all the glory. Amen.

Psalm 135:15-18

The idols of the nations are silver and gold, The work of men's hands. They have mouths, but they do not speak; Eyes they have, but they do not see; They have ears, but they do not hear; Nor is there any breath in their mouths. Those who make them are like them; So is everyone who trusts in them.

Father, all around me I see a world full of Your lost children and they are serving other gods. Lord, they worship their possessions, their entertainment, their bodies, and homes. Your people have turned to idols, but one day Lord, they will know that the things they serve are empty and bring no lasting joy. Father, I pray for them, open their eyes. Help Your children to see. Father God, send down Your Holy Spirit and bring revival fire to Your Church once again. Make us strong once more and help us to impact our communities. I pray for Your flock Lord Keep them clean and pure. Help them to burn bright for You in these dark times. Lord God, revive Your people.

178

Psalm 136:1
Oh, give thanks to the Lord, for He is good!
For His mercy endures forever.

Oh God, where would I be if You were like mere men? I would have been cast off long ago. Yet Your mercies endure forever. Your love never fails. You seek me out when I wander and stray. You call me home when I run away. In my zeal I may run too far ahead, but You remain patient with me. Whether I have fallen short or far, You continue to show Your mercy to me. I cannot earn Your love because You give it freely and abundantly. You pour out Your goodness upon me Lord. You protect me and You provide for me. How could I have ever sought after another? Why would I ever stray? You are so good Lord, and Your mercies endure forever.

Psalm 136:12-14
With a strong hand, and with an outstretched arm, For His mercy endures forever; To Him who divided the Red Sea in two, For His mercy endures forever; And made Israel pass through the midst of it, For His mercy endures forever;

Lord, You made a way when there was no way. Lord God, I never could have escaped my past by my own strength. It was by Your strength and Your hand that You led me in the way of salvation. Father, You came for me while I was still deep in sin. You called out to me and I came to You. LORD God, You parted the waters and opened the path for me. You are so good to me Lord. How ever can I describe it? Though I still wander and stray, You continually bring me home. Not only did You part the sea for me to enter in, but You closed it again behind me. You won't let me go back to that old life. And all of this, simply because You love me. Thank You Lord. Bless Your name.

Psalm 137:4-5

How shall we sing the Lord's song In a foreign land? If I forget you, O Jerusalem, Let my right hand forget its skill!

How is it Lord that I so quickly forget Your blessings? So often You pour out Your mercies upon me and then before I know it, I am in a new place, forgetting where You once had me. The cares and troubles of this world carry me away from You. Though I desire to sit at Your feet and learn from You, a myriad of distractions carry me away. Day by day I drift and then I wonder where You have gone? But You have never left me. I am the one who wanders away. Lord, let me never forget the great blessings that You pour out in me. Never let me forget the little things that I so easily take for granted. Keep my eyes on heaven and the great things that You have in store for those who love You.

Psalm 138:1-3

I will praise You with my whole heart; Before the gods I will sing praises to You. I will worship toward Your holy temple, And praise Your name For Your lovingkindness and Your truth; For You have magnified Your word above all Your name. In the day when I cried out, You answered me, And made me bold with strength in my soul.

Oh Lord, my God, You are amazing! I love You with all of my soul. While this whole world may fail me, You are faithful to me. I do not care what others may think of me, I want to praise You all day long. They do not know of Your greatness, they do not know of Your goodness. LORD God, You are great! And in Your Word I find You. Day by day I search and I see more of You. You reveal Yourself to me through Your Word and You show me what You desire of me. When I am in need of You, You speak to me through Your Word. When I need direction in life, Your Word shows me what I must do. Thank You for Your holy Word Father. And thank You for Your Word becoming flesh. Jesus, You are the mark which I strive for. You are my chief cornerstone which I build my life upon. I look to You Lord Jesus. Praise You!

Psalm 138:6

Though the Lord is on high, Yet He regards the lowly; But the proud He knows from afar.

Father God, I pray that You would help empty me of myself. Take away my prideful desires and fill me with Your humility. Help me to do great things in Your name, and turn all glory and praise to You. By the power of Your Holy Spirit, help me direct all glory and praise to Your Son Jesus. Remind me of my frailty. Remind me of the shortness of my life. Who am I, but a servant at Your disposal? I can bring nothing to come to pass, but You God, You can shake the mountains. Never let me become high in my own opinion. Keep me humble and keep me close to Your side.

Psalm 139:13-14

For You formed my inward parts; You covered me in my mother's womb. I will praise You, for I am fearfully and wonderfully made; Marvelous are Your works, And that my soul knows very well.

Lord God, even when I do not know where I am going and what I am doing, You have always known. You have always known me and the path that You have had in store for me. Even before I was born You were making things ready for me. You were setting things in motion to bring me to this day. God, I ask that You keep me in Your will and then You empower me to walk in Your ways. Help me to trust You and help me to listen to Your still small voice. Let me be sensitive to Your Holy Spirit. Let me seek Your direction in things both big and small. I know that You have a plan for me God. Help me to seek it out and follow it.

Psalm 139:1-3

O Lord, You have searched me and known me. You know my sitting down and my rising up; You understand my thought afar off. You comprehend my path and my lying down, And are acquainted with all my ways.

LORD God, it baffles my mind that You love me so much, even though You know the depths of my heart. I can hide nothing from You. I have never gotten away with anything. You have record of every word I have ever spoken and every thought that has passed through my mind. Knowing all this, You still love me and use me. You cleanse me and You help me be the person that I want to be. I can strive so hard to please You, yet either way, You still choose to love me. Your goodness knows no end Lord. You love me because of Your goodness. Thank You Lord for loving me in spite of all of my sin and shortcomings. Thank You for saving me and cleansing me. Thank You for being so good to a sinner like me.

Psalm 139:4

For there is not a word on my tongue, But behold, O Lord, You know it altogether.

Oh great all knowing God, what great comfort I find in Your power. Lord, long I have known that You see my every thought. You know my darkest secrets. You know the wickedness of my heart. But Lord, that is not all You see. You see my desire to be holy. You see my longing to be free from my sins. Lord, when I struggle to pray, You know that I am struggling. You know how desperately I desire to be better for You. God, You know that I am not just complacent. You know how weak I feel. You know how tired I feel. LORD God, help me to remember that You not only know my failures, but You also know my deepest desire, to love You more. God, take me by the hand and lead me to my next step. I am nothing without You God. I know it and You know it too.

Psalm 139:17-18

How precious also are Your thoughts to me, O God! How great is the sum of them! If I should count them, they would be more in number than the sand;

Oh my Lord, how great is Your love for me! If I could sing it, it would be a song without end. If I could comprehend it, I would know all things. Lord God, Your love is infinite towards Your servant. How could a holy God love a sinner like me? Because of Your goodness, Your mercy, and Your amazing grace. Your grace is unending and Your mercies are without number. As I rise and as I lay myself down to sleep, let me be thinking about Your great love for me. When others let me down, help me think of the One who gave His Son for me. Your goodness is beyond my comprehension Lord. I cannot grasp it, I cannot fathom it, and so I will just praise You. Your love, Oh God, is amazing and Your mercies endure forever!

Psalm 139:23-24

Search me, O God, and know my heart; Try me, and know my anxieties; And see if there is any wicked way in me, And lead me in the way everlasting.

Oh God, this is my prayer, search me deep within Lord. Search out my mind, my heart, and my soul. Search me in the secret places. Search every part of me where I may try to hide. Reveal to me what You find Lord. Reveal the sin, reveal the pride, and reveal the greed. Whatever You find, if it displeases You, show it to me. Address it and do not let me run from it. Help me to repent of those things You find and then lead me down the path of righteousness. Help me to walk in Your ways and give me Your peace that surpasses understanding. Lord God, I want to know that I am in Your will above all things. Above my happiness, above my comfort, above my preference, I want to know that I am serving You in spirit and in truth. Lead me in the way everlasting Lord. Help me to walk just as Your Son Jesus walked.

Psalm 139:7-10

*Where can I go from Your Spirit? Or where can I flee from
Your presence? If I ascend into heaven, You are there; If I
make my bed in hell, behold, You are there. If I take the
wings of the morning, And dwell in the uttermost parts of
the sea, Even there Your hand shall lead me, And Your right
hand shall hold me.*

It amazes me Lord, that I cannot run from You. Even when I
think that I am running from You, I find myself running to
Your arms. Why do I ever run? I become weak and angry.
Like a small child, I fight the One who loves me. But like a
loving Father, You let me kick, You let me scream, and once
I have calmed down You scoop me up in Your arms and You
remind me that while I may run, You never run. While I may
push away, You are always there for me. Help me to grow up
Lord. I don't want to run away from You ever again. Yet I
feel that at some point I will, but I know that once again,
You'll be right there to catch me in Your loving arms.

Psalm 140:6-7

*You are my God; Hear the voice of my supplications, O
LORD. O GOD the Lord, the strength of my salvation, You
have covered my head in the day of battle.*

Oh LORD God, You hear me when I call. My voice is never
unheard, nor are the thoughts of my heart a secret. You know
everything that I am facing and every fear I hold within. And
so, I pray for You to protect me, heal me, and guide me. Give
me the confidence that I long for to speak boldly on Your
behalf. Help me to boldly proclaim Your goodness to all
peoples. Lord I know that You will protect me as I go and
work on Your behalf. Let Your presence surround me as I
fight on Your behalf. Let all that I do Lord, be on Your
behalf. For I know that You will bless those who honor You
and You will protect those who do Your will. Keep me in
Your will Father. Lead me step by step.

Psalm 141:1-2

LORD, I cry out to You; Make haste to me! Give ear to my voice when I cry out to You. Let my prayer be set before You as incense, The lifting up of my hands as the evening sacrifice.

Lord God, here I am! Here I am God. Take all of me now. I am here before You asking You to have Your way in me. Hear my voice as I cry out to You LORD God. You are my God! You are my King! I pray that my life brings You great joy. I pray that You find my works pleasant before Your eyes. Lord, I give myself as a sacrifice to You. Take my life and all that I bring and use it for Your glory. Let me draw all peoples to You. Let my life be a light to those around me. Help me to live for You my Lord. I love You and desire to bring You praise. Amen.

Psalm 141:3-4

Set a guard, O LORD, over my mouth; Keep watch over the door of my lips. Do not incline my heart to any evil thing, To practice wicked works With men who work iniquity; And do not let me eat of their delicacies.

Oh LORD, watch over me day by day. Though I long to serve you from the depths of my soul, the world continues to try to draw me back. Old ways, old habits, and old desires come creeping in after long being forgotten. I did not think that they would ever come back, but they do. Do not let me sink back into the place You pulled me from Lord. I have no desire to go back. Renew my heart each day to long after Your ways and Your Truth. Wash me by Your Word and refresh my soul. Protect me from the temptations of this age and keep me going down the path You have set me on.

Psalm 141:8-10

But my eyes are upon You, O GOD the Lord; In You I take refuge; Do not leave my soul destitute. Keep me from the snares they have laid for me, And from the traps of the workers of iniquity. Let the wicked fall into their own nets, While I escape safely.

As the troubles of this world surround me, my eyes on are You Lord. When there seems to be no options left to turn to, let me keep my focus on You and Your good plans for me. And when all hope seems lost, let me find my hope in You. I want You to be the place that I find peace. I desire to find security in knowing that You are my God and You only have good plans for me. Help me to obey Your desires for me Lord. When the enemy desires to get me off track, help me keep my focus in Your great strength. Do not let me trust in my own strength, it will always fail me. Let me trust in You and You alone Lord. You are my Rock and my Salvation.

Psalm 142:1-2

I cry out to the LORD with my voice; With my voice to the LORD I make my supplication. I pour out my complaint before Him; I declare before Him my trouble.

Father God, hear my heart and hear my needs. Lord, You know what I face and what my struggles are. You know all things. But hear me Lord! Let me pour out my heart to You. As a loving Father, hear Your child cry out to You. I need You Lord. I need Your help and Your assurance. Be my wonderful counselor and my strong tower. I don't want to turn to other people or other things. Let me find all of my strength in You. You are my hiding place, Oh Lord. I rest in You and I trust in You. Praise You Father, praise You.

Psalm 142:3

When my spirit was overwhelmed within me, Then You knew my path. In the way in which I walk They have secretly set a snare for me.

Oh Lord, my heart is troubled. Anxiety wells up within me. Anxiety wells up within me. It feels as if walls surround me. I call out to You, but cannot discern Your response. Lord, even when You are silent, I know that Your Word remains steadfast. Even in the times when I cannot hear You, Your Word changes not. You have always known that this day would come and You have guided me every step of the way up until this point. Help me to trust that Your plan will not fail. You know where I should go and what I should do. Let me walk by faith and trust that You will guide my steps. Lead me Lord by Your Spirit and Your Word. Keep me plodding along this path which You have placed me on. God, give me faith. Give me a simple and beautiful faith which I can walk by. Step by step You lead me. No matter what snare may lay before me, You will guide my steps. Yes Lord, You will lead and guide me as You always have. You have never failed me and You never will. If God is for us, who can be against us? Thank You Lord for being You. You are a wonderful Father and an amazing God. I love You, forever and ever, amen.

Psalm 143:1-2

Hear my prayer, O LORD, Give ear to my supplications! In Your faithfulness answer me, And in Your righteousness. Do not enter into judgment with Your servant, For in Your sight no one living is righteous.

Oh LORD, help me to remember how freely You give Your grace to me. Lord, no one is righteous in Your eyes. We have all fallen short of Your glory. Yet You choose to love us anyway. I cannot earn Your love, it is freely given. I cannot lose Your love because I never obtained it in the first place. You just poured it out on me freely. I'll never be good enough for You, but You will forever be good enough for me. Hear my prayers Lord! I come again to You needy and weak. Tell me what Your will is for me Father. Though I will never be righteous in Your eyes, I will keep striving to please You with me life. I give myself as an offering to You Lord. Be pleased with Your servant. Amen.

Psalm 143:8

Cause me to hear Your lovingkindness in the morning, For in You do I trust; Cause me to know the way in which I should walk, For I lift up my soul to You.

Father God, let Your Holy Spirit surround me with Your presence. Let me feel You moving within my being. I want to know that You are near. And I want to know that I am within Your will Father. God, I trust Your guidance and Your plans for me. Show me how to live, how to walk, and how to act. Guide me in all of my ways and let me always be leaning on Your Spirit for guidance. Lord God, I lift up my soul to You and my life to You. Have Your way in me Father. Do as You will. I trust You!

Psalm 143:10

Teach me to do Your will, For You are my God; Your Spirit is good. Lead me in the land of uprightness.

God, there is no greater desire in me than to be pleasing in Your sight. Before all else, I want Your approval. Lord, teach me to do Your will! If I wander, correct me quickly. Do not let me drift off Your path that You have set before me. You are my God and I trust You. Your Holy Spirit is my teacher and my guide. He goes before me and sweeps up after me. Lead me God! Speak to my heart and show me Your will for my life. As choices come before me, day by day, whisper in my ear what You desire for me to do. Lead me in the paths of righteousness, for Your name's sake.

Psalm 143:11

Revive me, O LORD, for Your name's sake! For Your righteousness' sake bring my soul out of trouble.

Oh Lord, create a revival in my heart. Set a fire in my soul that burns with zeal for Your holy name. Let me point others to You and live a life that brings glory to You. Let all that I do be for Your name's sake! Lord, if I ever stumble and fall, bring me back for Your name's sake. Correct me and rebuke me if need be. I do not want to bring dishonor to Your name. Let my life only be pleasing before Your eyes. Oh Lord, I know You will defend me. You will fight on my behalf. I put You in charge of my battles. Do not let me fight in my own strength. Let me look to You for all my strength and power. You are my great king. Revive me Lord, revive me.

Psalm 144:1
Blessed be the LORD my Rock, Who trains my hands for war, And my fingers for battle—

Thank You God, You are so good to me. You have plans for me. Plans that You have been preparing me for. Oh, why have I ever doubted Your goodness? Through trials I questioned You, yet You always had me in Your hands. You were testing me, strengthening me, and proving me. You knew the things that I needed to grow in and so You made me struggle and grow stronger. But Lord, You are my Rock. You have brought me to this place today and I am stronger because of the work You have done in me. You lead me by Your strong hand and You take me down the path that brings me to where I need to go. I would not have taken that path on my own, but in Your goodness and in Your wisdom, You took me down that path that brings You glory. Praise You Father. Thank You. Hallelujah.

Psalm 144:3
LORD, what is man, that You take knowledge of him? Or the son of man, that You are mindful of him?

Oh Lord God, who am I? Who am I that You should love me so? What have I done to earn Your great favor? I have done nothing! I have never been worthy of Your great love, but You love me anyway. I fail time and time again, but Your goodness to me is without fail. You swoop down and pick me up when I fall. You became a man, took on a body of flesh, and died on my behalf! Who am I Lord? I'm just Your humble servant. I'm not worthy to sit at the King's feet, yet You prepare me a throne. I'm taken aback by You. Your love reaches down from heaven and lifts me up. Your mercy is without end and knows no bounds. While You hold the galaxy in motion, You also know the hairs on my head. You are a great God and a God worthy to be praised. I love You Lord. Thank You for thinking of me,
Your humble servant.

Psalm 144:15
Happy are the people who are in such a state; Happy are the people whose God is the LORD!

Lord, You make me happy. So simple and so true, You bring me joy. This world offers many temporary things, but You give me something eternal. You give me life everlasting, but even more so, You call me by name. You know me and You love me. Lord, Your goodness brings a smile to my face. There, in the quiet place, Your still small voice whispers to me. I hear You call out to me with Your loving voice. You draw me near and You comfort me with Your kind words. Lord, being in Your presence is like nothing this world could ever offer. Help me to always be by Your side. And help me show others the great goodness of the Lord God Almighty. Let me share Your peace with this world. It so needs it Father. One day everyone will know Your great joy, but until that time, use me to share it with others. Use me to accomplish Your will Lord.
I am happy to do it.

Psalm 145:2
Every day I will bless You, And I will praise Your name forever and ever.

Oh LORD, while I waver to and fro, You are unchangeable. I drift at times. I swing from hot to cold. But you God, You never change. You are the same yesterday, today, and forever more. And some days my heart is colder than others. I feel as if You are distant, but I know that You have not moved, it is only I who drift away. Lord, keep me from wandering. Help me to remain steadfast in my time with You. Even on the days when I do not feel Your presence, help me to seek You. Daily let me come to You, my King, to seek Your face. God, when my flesh is weak, remember that my spirit is willing. Help me to be strong and seek You in the times when I struggle. Help me to seek You when my hope is lost. Help me to seek You daily and to have open ears and an open heart to hear what Your will is for me each day. Help me seek You daily Father because I love You. Amen.

Psalm 145:3
Great is the LORD, and greatly to be praised;
And His greatness is unsearchable.

God, You never cease to amaze me. My knowledge of You grows deeper and deeper and You always have something new for me. God, You are unsearchable, and Your ways are far above my ways. God, I find peace in worshipping the unsearchable God of all comfort. You have plans that I could never comprehend. Plans to prosper me and to grow me more into the image of Your Son Jesus. Lord Jesus, help me keep my eyes fixed upon You and Your great love for me. Thank You for the cross and all that You've done for me. Fill me with Your Spirit and help me to walk in truth. Oh Lord, Your Word is truth. Teach me Your unsearchable truths found in Your Word and help me to live by them day by day. Thank You Lord. Thank You.

Psalm 145:8-9
The LORD is gracious and full of compassion, Slow to anger and great in mercy. The LORD is good to all, And His tender mercies are over all His works.

Oh Father, how can You have patience for one like me? Your mercies are so unending. They never fail me, even though I fail them often. Your grace is abounding towards me and You are so very good to me. What have I done to deserve Your great love? Nothing. There is nothing that I could ever do to earn the love You have for me. Yet You love me anyway. Thank You Lord for pouring out Your great love on me. Thank You for being so good to me. Thank You for never changing. And thank You for Your Son. Amen.

Psalm 145:18

The LORD is near to all who call upon Him,
To all who call upon Him in truth.

Lord, You hear me when I call. I have never cried out without
You hearing my cries. I have never been alone. For You have
always been with me and You have promised to never leave nor
forsake me. Lord God, I pray that You would lead others into
this wonderful relationship with You. They say that they seek
You, yet they do not find You. Lord, they do not seek You in
truth! They desire to find a god of their own liking, but they
reject You for who You are. Lord, have mercy on them and
draw them to You. Open their eyes to the error of their ways and
help lead them to Your truth. Your Word is truth. God, I pray
that Your Word would impact their hard hearts and that they
would receive Your Spirit. That You would give them a new
heart and take their hearts of stone. God, You are near. Show
Yourself to them.

Psalm 146:3-4

Do not put your trust in princes, Nor in a son of man, in
whom there is no help. His spirit departs, he returns to his
earth; In that very day his plans perish.

Father, I live in a land of opportunities and options. And
though I am grateful that You have placed me here, the
world tries to lure me away with its temptations and reason.
Every man and thing tries to give me alternatives to You,
but I desire You and You alone. Help me to not trust in
doctors alone. Help me not to trust in my retirement alone.
Help me to not trust in my government or even my friends if
it means that I lose my trust in You. I want You to be the
first place that I turn for help. The first one whom I seek.
Thank You Lord for giving me all these good things, but do
not let me trust in them. I neither trust in horses, nor
chariots, nor cars, nor banks. I trust in You alone. While the
stock market may fail, and even my government ultimately
fall, You, O God, will never fail. Hallelujah.

Psalm 147:4-5

He counts the number of the stars; He calls them all by name. Great is our Lord, and mighty in power; His understanding is infinite.

How come the heathen cannot comprehend Your greatness? How come they question what they cannot understand? God, You are so far above us, forbid me that I ever try to comprehend You. Your ways are above my ways. Your thoughts are light years above my own. How could I ever fit You into my finite brain? God I cannot even count a small number of the stars, yet You count them and know them by name! Your understanding and Your power are greater than I could ever know. Lord, let me remain humbly at Your feet. Let me never become full of myself and help me to remain full of Your Spirit. I bow before You. You are great, my Lord, my King. Remember me, Your humble servant. Again Lord, I bow before You. Praise Your holy name. Amen

Psalm 147:11

The LORD takes pleasure in those who fear Him, In those who hope in His mercy.

Father, as the day goes by, I often drift from Your presence. I start so strong and think of You as I seek You in the morning. Person by person whom I see I slowly lose my focus on Your presence. And before I know it, I find myself in the flesh. I lose my reverence for You. I do not treat Your children with the tender love that I ought to. I do not fear for the sake of lost souls as I know I should. Help me keep my reverent heart ablaze as the day goes by. Help me to never lose focus of the eternal calling that You have placed on my life. Help me to be ready to give an answer to all those who seek it. An answer for that great hope You have given me. You bless me so much Lord. I only desire to offer You something back in return. So I give You my heart and my life. I pray that all that I do is a sweet aroma before You. I love You Lord.

Psalm 148:4-5

Praise Him, you heavens of heavens, And you waters above the heavens! Let them praise the name of the LORD, For He commanded and they were created.

Lord God, Your power knows no bounds. What You have done, by the simplest of means, blows my mind. You spoke and it was done. What the scientists of earth have spent centuries trying to comprehend, You simply made by the word of Your command. How great and awesome is our God! Lord, You have all power. You have all might. You are sovereign over all Your creation. One day every knee will bow and one day You will rid this world of Satan and sin. Lord, I thank You for Your great love. In all of Your wondrous creation, You still have time to think of me. Lord, I am but a small part in Your great plan, but You know the number of hairs on my head. Thank You Lord for loving me so much. I am unworthy of Your amazing grace. Thank You Lord. Amen.

Psalm 148:13

Let them praise the name of the LORD, For His name alone is exalted; His glory is above the earth and heaven.

You and You alone, oh God, deserve all my attention and praise. Before friends, and even family, You should be my greatest joy. Above all the things of the earth, my heart should long for Your presence. Oh God, be the king of my heart and the ruler over all my life. Be glorified through all that I do. Let Your name be magnified and let my heart never turn to another. Oh, how fickle my heart can be, yet Your love is ever faithful. Oh, how quickly I become distracted by the things of this earth, yet I am forever under Your direct care. Lord, my fickleness is perfectly contrasted by Your great faithfulness. Oh, how I love You, Almighty God, maker of heaven and earth. My Savior, my King, and the lover of my soul. Praise Your name forever.

Psalm 149:1

Praise the LORD! Sing to the LORD a new song, And His praise in the assembly of saints.

Praise You Lord, Praise You. You are amazing. Your goodness knows no end. Your mercies are beyond measure. Your love abounds! I cannot help but praise Your great name. I was a sinner, wretched and lost, but You found me and You restored me. While I was still sinning, You showed Your great love towards me. You have given me Your Spirit to lead me and to guide me. You cleanse me day by day. More and more You conform me into the image of Your Son, King Jesus. I have done nothing to deserve this great love. Yet You pour it out all the more abundantly. Your salvation is strong and true. All I have is Yours Father. Take my life and let it be, wholly consecrated unto You Lord God. All I have is Yours. I am Yours. Hallelujah, praise be to Your great name.

Psalm 150:1

Praise the LORD! Praise God in His sanctuary; Praise Him in His mighty firmament!

Lord, let my life be a song to You. With every gift You have given me, let me sing Your praise. Lord, let my feet dance for You. Let me arms be lifted high in Your praise. Let me hands do the works You have set before them. Father God, let my knees be humbly bowed before You. Let no wicked thing come before my eyes and let no evil proceed from my mouth. Let Your praises flow freely from my tongue. God, have my ears be always listening for the direction of Your Holy Spirit. I want to give You all that I am Lord. Let my life be a living sacrifice, continually before You. Transform me into an instrument that is only used to fulfill Your perfect will here on earth. LORD God, You are my all and my everything. Take me Lord. Receive me into Your kingdom. I am humbly and forever Yours. Amen.

ABOUT THE AUTHOR

Joseph Edwards-Hoff was raised near Seattle, Washington. While raised in the church, it was at college that he gave his life to the Lord and began down a road of learning and growing in Him. While in college he met his wife Nicole and they were married in 2009. They currently have 6 children: Haley, Judah, Jubilee, Benaiah, Hannah, and Elianna.

In 2014 Joe was called into pastoral ministry in the town that he was teaching public school in. The family moved there and eventually he became the pastor of the Revival Church in Grandview, Washington. There at his church he spends his time trying to help other believers grow in God's Word, seek the fullness of God's Spirit, and to seek Him in prayer.

Printed in Great Britain
by Amazon

16769637R00115